LUCKY TWICE

DEBRA WEISSMAN SEAMAN

Lucky Twice

Published by Jacobs Writing Consultants, LLC
www.Jacobswc.com

ISBN: 978-1-943157-71-6
Printed in the United States of America

For more information, go to:
www.luckytwice.net

Dedication

We would like to dedicate this book to our former spouses, Janice and Paul. Our lives would not be where they are without them. They are loved and deeply missed.

Acknowledgments

I would also like to thank Sharon Gutterman, PhD, for being a true and dear friend for over ten years. She has supported me through all my highs and lows. Not only is she a dear friend, but she is an inspiring speaker of Mindfulness, stress reduction, and well-being. She has helped so many people from the likes of physicians at Yale University to inmates in correctional institutions. She can help many people with their day to day stress, and she has always been supportive of me during all my struggles and achievements. If you want to reach out to Sharon, her website is www.mindfulwow.com.

Special Thanks

Allen and I would like to thank Judi, Allen's sister, and his friend, Lavonne. Lavonne not only helped Allen when he lost Janice but coaxed him into joining Our Time dating service.

We'd also like to thank Our Time dating service, for without them Allen and I would have never met.

We'd like to thank all of our family and friends who helped us get through difficult times and stood by us as we moved on with our new chapter in life.

Finally, we would like to thank Kathleen and Tim of Jacobs Writing Consultants for helping us write our story. Everyone told us we had a wonderful story and should write a book, but it would have never come to fruition without them.

Table of Contents

Debbie's Story ...

Debbie & Allen's First Date: *Her Side*

I always told Paul, my husband of thirty-five years, "If I die and you meet someone new – get married. Don't be alone." But I always added one condition. "Just make sure you don't give that bitch one more cent than you would give me."

He would never reciprocate; maybe he couldn't bear to imagine me in the arms of another man. Even when he was diagnosed with cancer, he couldn't bring himself to say the same to me. It wasn't until he was in hospice, three days before his death, that he gave me the gift: permission to remarry.

"Don't be alone," he begged me. "Promise me, please."

Looking back, I think it was his words that gave me the courage to remarry.

Six months after losing Paul, I met Allen, the perfect man for me in every way. Things were moving quickly between us, and we were starting to talk marriage. But I soon developed cold feet and was ready to throw it all away. I was bogged down with guilt. To be so incredibly happy simply felt like I was betraying the only man I had ever been with. I was hoping to wait at least a year out of respect to Paul and everyone else in my life. But I was so lonely, and Allen came into my life sooner than I ever expected. I couldn't bring Paul back, and realized for the first time in my life, it doesn't matter what other people thought. If they didn't approve, it was their problem, not mine. I just needed to be happy. It was my memory of Paul's blessing, that selfless gift, which helped me to move forward.

This is a story of losing everything you hold dear. It is a story of finding yourself alone in the world, staying strong, and finding love again. In a few short years, I lost not only Paul, but both of my dear parents.

Paul had been battling cancer for nine years. When the end came near, he wanted us to move to Southwest Florida, where he could enjoy the balmy weather and the comfort of the ocean in his final days. My mother was also battling cancer at the time. As I was the primary caregiver for both of them, I found myself flying back and forth from Connecticut to Naples. It was then Paul and I rented in Sarasota, Florida so we could be closer to my mother and see if it was to our liking. Paul loved the area so much, we built a home in Naples. As difficult as that move was for me, I was truly happy that he got to spend his last days in the sunshine state.

Fourteen months later, shortly after my mother succumbed to her illness, I lost Paul. To add to this heartache, my father's health was failing, and I was preparing for my own heart surgery. Yet through it all, I was able to hold it together and stay strong.

In order to deal with all of this heartache, I kept myself busy. I joined several women's groups where I made some terrific friends, but it didn't change the fact that every night I went home alone. Even with my dog for a companion, the house felt empty. Feeling lonely, I finally gave in to the urging of a concerned friend and joined Our Time, a dating website for the fifty and over community.

It had been less than a year since Paul's death. I felt I wasn't ready for anything serious, but I thought it would be fun to just go out on dates and meet different men. As it turns out, that's not really who I am; I knew I wanted to be with just one man. But of course, he had to be the right man, and it would be a tall order to find a man as good as Paul was.

For some time, I was talking to two gentlemen from the dating site, but I hadn't taken the plunge and gone out on a date with either one of them. After hearing "horror" stories from friends who have met men online, I quickly learned the world of dating had drastically changed. It had evolved from "can I carry your books" to "your place or mine?" I'm glad I held out; it was as if someone was watching out for me.

One day in late October, I came across Allen's profile. He was a handsome man with a full head of gorgeous salt and pepper hair, and I was intrigued. But what really drew me to him was the fact that he was a widower rather than a divorcee. Here was someone, like me, who had been in a loving, long-term marriage. He knew what it took to be in a committed relationship and to lose their spouse to cancer.

The fact that he was 6'2" didn't hurt either. Being 5'8", it seemed I was always the tall one. Even in high school I was always the tallest in my class and thought it would be wonderful to be with someone who was at least six foot.

I sent him a message with a simple "Hi," and our communication started. We hit it off from the start and continued to message each other for several weeks. Still, I was cautious. I wasn't ready to give him my number just yet. When I finally did, he wasted no time in asking me for some "nice" pictures.

"Nice pictures? What do you mean?" I laughed, purposely misunderstanding him. "I'm not sending you nude pictures of myself!"

"Oh, no, no, no. That's not what I meant," he replied.

So I sent him one of me in a bathing suit. He must have loved it because we had our first date soon after.

We decided to meet on December 31. If all went well, we would be ushering in the New Year together. It seemed like the perfect way to mark our first date.

At the risk of sounding forward, I invited Allen to stay the night. I didn't want him driving all the way home to Cape Coral, some fifty-five miles away, with all the drunks on the road. "I know you're going to think I'm crazy," I told him, "but pack a bag and stay over."

I have a good sense of character; so, if something about Allen seemed out of place, I would end the date early. Plus, I was smart and did a background check on him. He had no criminal history; everything he told me about himself was true. He really did have a wife who he lost to cancer. His work history matched up as well. Yet, all of this didn't quell my nervousness about going out on a date. Imagine for a moment you are fifty-seven going on your first date since you were eighteen years old. It's enough to make anyone apprehensive.

We arranged to meet for brunch in old Naples, a beachside town with its own unique charm. Even though I had been living in Naples for over a year, I hadn't had the chance to explore it because of Paul's illness. Everything was still new to me. So, when a friend recommended Jane's on Third, promising me the food would be delicious, it seemed like a good choice.

I arrived in my new Kia and waited outside the quaint-looking restaurant. I kept an eye out for Allen. I'm not sure how I missed this, but Allen was standing on the sidewalk checking me out. He later confessed that if he didn't like the looks of me, he was going to leave and go back home. But when I turned around, I caught him smiling down at me. I blurted out loud, "Is that you?" I guess my voice was off or cracked or something, because he still likes to tease me about it.

The hostess seated us outside near a pond. My anxiety must have shown because Allen kept touching my arm and telling me to relax. His sweetness and good humor soon won me over, and I began to calm down. After brunch, we walked hand in hand down to the Naples pier. It all felt so natural. The date was a wonderful blur of walking on the beach, conversation, coffee, and ice cream.

It seemed too good to be true. But it was all true, because as I mentioned before, I believe someone was watching out for me...or maybe two someones. We often joke that Paul and Janice (Allen's deceased wife) must have been looking down on us on that first date, probably having a good laugh too. In fact, we talked about them right off the bat. It feels like they have always been an important part of our relationship.

Sometimes, when Allen is teasing me, I walk over to Janice's picture and ask her how she put up with him for so long, and Allen will do the same to Paul's picture. I think that's one of the things that is truly great about our relationship. We are not forbidden to talk about the past. We both have fond memories of our spouses, and it would be horrible to have to keep those memories to ourselves. I know that would not necessarily be the case if either of us had ended up with someone else. When someone has gone through a difficult divorce, bitterness and negativity will sometimes linger into a second marriage.

We weren't the only ones to notice we were having a grand old time on the pier. There was a young woman in her twenties who was walking on the boardwalk. She must have walked past us five or six times when she approached us and said, "You guys are adorable and so in love." Of course she didn't realize Allen and I had just met four hours earlier. She took our picture using my cell phone saying, "Oh my God, you are the most adorable couple."

One thing we can say about our first date is that fireworks went off – literally. Collier County celebrated New Year's Eve by shooting fireworks over the Gulf Coast, and we had front row seats. Allen's favorite holiday is the 4th of July, and he was really looking forward to watching the fireworks on the beach with me. However, the booming was quite loud in my opinion, and we ended up leaving early.

Allen's friend, Lavonne, who works as a counselor, and his sister, Judi, knew all about our plans for the evening. They gave him this advice: "If you really like Debbie and you sleep over, be sure to lock the guest bedroom when you go to bed." I found this to be hilarious because usually that advice is given to a woman.

Now Allen's favorite joke is telling the story of how I banged on the door all night because I wanted to get in, but really it was my dog who was scratching on the door. I think she wanted to cuddle with her new friend.

The next day, after breakfast, Allen did go home, but afterward, we were on the phone morning, noon, and night, like teenagers back when we had landline phones. By the third day, we were inseparable.

Growing Up

In 1959, my overjoyed parents welcomed me into the world. My father was a salesman for a Buick dealership, and my mother worked for Rhode Island College in the admissions office.

Little did they know when they brought me home to our modest Rhode Island house that I'd be their only surviving child. They were planning on having more children, but my mother would ultimately suffer three miscarriages.

At age six, I was woken in the middle of the night and shipped off to my aunt's house, where I would stay for the next few days. I had no idea what was going on or even where my parents were. Years later, I learned they had gone to the hospital to deliver their second child. Unfortunately, the baby was stillborn. I realized, as I got older, that my mom must have suffered for a very long time after that. I don't know if she had a nervous breakdown, but I do know it must have been devastating for her to come home to an empty nursery she had spent months decorating.

Growing up, everybody felt sorry for me because I was an only child. A question I was often asked was, "Do you mind not having a sister or brother?"

My response was always the same: "I have nothing to compare it to." I couldn't miss what I didn't know. Besides, I had a happy childhood with loving parents and lots of good memories.

One particular memory is my mother hiding candy before going out to play cards with her friends. As soon as she was gone, my father would look at me and I'd look at him.

"Come on," he'd say, grabbing my arm. "Let's find the candy."

My mother would come home and yell at us good naturedly, "You ate the candy!"

I had a large extended family, complete with grandparents, aunts, uncles, and cousins who would come over every weekend to play cards. There was always lots of fun and laughter.

There was also Rhonda, my best friend since birth. Our mothers were good friends and their mothers were best friends, so we naturally followed suit. Three generations of best friends! Rhonda and I lived in different towns, but we went to summer camp together. We were inseparable on weekends and after school.

One other thing I remember about school was that I learned I needed eye glasses. I probably needed them from the day I was born, but it took my first-grade teacher telling my parents that I couldn't see the blackboard.

By the time I started junior high, I was one of the tallest kids and became a target. I was tall, lanky, and bespectacled. Because Lisa, another friend of mine, was short and heavy, the other kids dubbed us the Odd Couple. We got picked on all the time, but the bullying was a lot worse for her. I think the difference was that she cried while she was being teased. I stood my ground. I wouldn't give them the satisfaction of seeing me cry, so they picked on me less. In fact, the bullying became so intolerable for Lisa she ended up transferring to another school. It was a terrible situation back then because the school system didn't have an anti-bullying campaign in place.

Even though I hated going to school, I hung in there. But soon it began to take a toll on me, and I lost all interest in my classes. However, when my grades began to slip, it didn't seem to worry my parents.

If I came home with a C, they'd tell me, "Yay! Good girl!"

They never encouraged me to go further and were always happy with what I did. Sometimes I wonder how far I might have gone if they had pushed me, but I have no regrets and feel blessed that they provided me with such a loving home. Still, as anyone who's ever been bullied can attest to, it didn't take away from the fact that it was an awful stage in my life. Luckily, things would turn around for me in high school.

It all started with a girl from my old neighborhood. We had lived on the same street and used to play together. We became good friends until we moved and lost touch with one another. Even though I hadn't seen her in years, we were able to rekindle our friendship once we entered high school.

She was a beautiful cheerleader dating the captain of the football team, but when she saw me in the halls she said, "Debbie!" And we instantly clicked.

Here I was, the Ugly Duckling, friends with the gorgeous girl everybody wanted to be with. She took me under her wing, and all of a sudden everybody accepted me. Now that I was no longer being picked on, I began to relax and actually enjoy school. Although I wouldn't say my high school teachers exactly inspired me, they were nice and I liked them all.

I started to become involved with several after-school activities. I joined the Spanish Club and took modern dance and mixed choir. Our high school had a little newspaper called *The Thunderbolt*, which came out once a week, and I was in charge of distribution.

When I turned sixteen, my older cousin purchased a new vehicle and gave me her used one. My first car was a big, beautiful '66 Buick Skylark. I loved it.

I also joined a youth organization with Rhonda. The meetings were held in Warwick, and I would drive to the synagogue every weekend.

Rhonda and I became very active with the group and joined many of the committees. We were in charge of correspondence, and one of our responsibilities was putting out the newsletter. I enjoyed writing the articles because it brought out my creative side. Besides being a lot of fun, it was the first time in my life I thought I could be a writer.

Back then there were no computers, so we mailed the issues to the 200 or so people in the group. On Friday nights, we would follow up by calling everybody to remind them of the upcoming activities.

"Okay, don't forget, we have apple picking tomorrow," we'd say. Or we'd remind them of whatever event was going on.

I was still tall and skinny, but the guys were catching up fast. It was within this social group that I started dating. Everything was so innocent back then. I met many wonderful people and developed strong friendships. I was blossoming.

That summer my cousin got me my first job at the Musical Tent, a theater in the round. There was a different performer every week; it was quite the lineup with many famous acts such as Don Rickles, Tom Jones, and The Carpenters.

As a popcorn girl, I worked alongside six or seven other girls. We wore little blue uniforms with white nylons. During intermission, we'd serve the people at the concession stand. The owners ran a catering company, so when the theater closed for the season, they asked me to work for them after school and on the weekends. I enjoyed making the sandwiches, potato and macaroni salads, and desserts so much that I continued working for them even after I started college. It's where I developed my love of cooking and baking.

My parents loved baking and cooking too, and you'd always find the three of us in the kitchen arguing.

My dad would say, "You don't need a recipe."

My mother and I would reply, "Yes, we do."

He would counter with, "Add a little of this. Do a little of that."

We would respond, "No, you have to follow the recipe!"

We were always laughing. Always.

I was extremely close to my parents. My mother was my best friend and was sweet as pie. She was a peace-loving woman who never bothered anybody or created problems. My father was more like an older brother to me, but because we were very similar, we would sometimes butt heads. We did everything together, so I think it hurt him when I wanted to go out and be with my friends.

Even though I was good and never got into any real trouble, he wasn't ready to let go of his baby girl. "Stay home with the family," he would say. "We'll have fun."

"Dad, I need a life," I would tell him.

Every year, we took a vacation at the Rhode Island shore, renting a small cottage. My mother would take the month of August off and my dad would commute because he had to keep working.

We would also spend a week in Cape Cod, staying in Hyannis every year. I was impressed that the hotel had an indoor swimming pool. We would walk to the restaurants in the small downtown area. It never deviated. My parents never went far from home; they just weren't into traveling. So, it's surprising that I would one day become a world traveler.

College & Meeting Paul

I met Paul at the University of Rhode Island on the first day of school. As we stood outside the lecture hall waiting to enter our first class of the term, I struck up a conversation. We hit it off, discovering we were in four out of five classes together. I was studying business with a minor in management, and Paul was a business major with a minor in economics. One of the more interesting courses we were taking was computer science. Personal computers were starting to make their debut, and we were excited about the endless opportunities this technology represented.

We became close friends and spent lots of time with each other, not only in the classroom but outside as well. At the end of the day, we'd go back to my dorm and talk for hours on end. Paul was brilliant; blessed with an incredible memory, he earned straight A's even though he never cracked open a book.

I would prove harder to crack, however. Paul fell for me hard and wanted more than a friendship, but I turned him down because I was already dating someone else. I met Scott when I was sixteen and fell madly in love. Even though he was in the next state over studying at Boston University,

I was fiercely loyal to him because I thought we'd end up marrying.

This rejection proved too much for Paul. Besides not being able to get his girl, his classes were not challenging him. Miserable, he transferred to Rutgers University.

Knowing we would miss each other's friendship, we vowed to stay in touch. Back then, talking long distance on the phone could really add up. And as most people still did not own a personal computer, we stayed in touch via the old-fashioned way: by writing letters. We both kept everything. I'm happy to report, I still have every card, letter, and "miss you" note to this day.

At the end of my freshman year, Scott came down from Massachusetts and broke up with me because he had met somebody else.

I was devastated.

Paul was always in the back of my mind, and I knew deep down he was the one for me, but I wasn't ready to put my heart out there just yet. Needing time to heal, I dated several guys during my sophomore year, but there always seemed to be something lacking. I came to realize what it was...they weren't Paul.

I took matters into my own hands and decided to call him. The only problem was that his family's number was unlisted. Luckily, I remembered they owned and operated Weissman and Sons, a wholesale meat company. Believe it or not, they were a Jewish family dealing in pork.

During summers and vacation breaks, Paul worked in the office for his grandfather Albert Weissman.

"I'm a friend of Paul Weissman," I told the person on the other end of the phone. "Is there any way you could give me his home phone number?"

She seemed doubtful as to who I was, but to my relief, she gave me his number.

"You're calling me?" Paul asked when I finally got him on the phone.

"Yeah," I said. "What are you doing next weekend?"

"Just tell me when and where," he said, "and I'll be there."

Thank God – he was still available. He had been sitting on his front porch with a few friends that summer night when I called. Years later, his friends told me that Paul was grinning from ear to ear when he hung up.

Paul drove down in his brand new '78 Nova, a cute little blue car. He was wearing ripped jeans and a t-shirt with The Nets written across a giant basketball. I took one look at his long Brillo-y red hair, which made him look like he had just stepped off of a motorcycle, and thought my parents were going to throw him out of the house. I was wrong. They loved him and thought he was the sweetest guy. In fact, they liked him so much they let us stay in their finished basement – complete with a bedroom, bathroom, and den – once we became more serious.

"Go ahead, both of you stay downstairs," they told us.

Not too many parents would do that, especially in that day and age. I figured they'd rather have us be safe and not in the back of a car or God knows where.

We spent as much time together as possible. When summer ended, Paul went back to New Jersey while I stayed in Rhode Island. We did our best to schedule our classes from Tuesdays to Thursdays so that we could spend long weekends together. We kept Amtrak in business traveling back and forth. Paul had his own place on campus, but hated it. Eventually he moved back home and commuted to school.

Six months after we started dating, Paul proposed. He was an avid Bruce Springsteen fan, and we were laying on his bed listening to the *Born to Run* album. Ironically, the song playing was "She's the One."

He turned to me and said, "Will you marry me?"

I didn't even need to think about it for a half a second and could only reply, "YES!"

We were so much in love. There was no question that I wanted to spend the rest of my life with him. It seemed natural and perfect. We graduated in May 1981, and married in September of that year. We were the first of all our friends to marry. We knew we were young, but didn't want to be separated one more day than we had to.

Wedding & Honeymoon

Our engagement lasted eighteen months because we wanted to finish college at our respective schools. Prior to finishing school, Paul was recruited by Mutual Benefit Life. He attended my graduation in May of 1981, and two weeks later I went to his. Not long afterward, he started work. Then we started our life together.

Paul was a huge Mets fan. His childhood bedroom was painted royal blue and had a shaggy orange carpet. Even his bar mitzvah party was decorated with the Mets colors.

"Your wedding colors should be blue and orange," Paul's friends would tease me.

"No, no," I laughed. But after thinking it over, I said, "You know, the bridesmaids' gowns could be apricot and the tuxedos a light blue."

In 1981, colored tuxedos were all the rage. Ordering blue and orange flowers was the easy part, and a Mets wedding was born. We got married over Labor Day weekend at the Temple Beth Torah, just a five-minute walk from my house. Of course, I wasn't going to walk in my wedding gown, but I decided against renting a limo for such a short distance. Paul's parents had just bought us a brand-new car as a wedding gift, and our friends were planning on writing "just married" on the back of it. But I thought they shouldn't do that!

Since I still had my 1966 Buick Skylark, I decided to let them decorate that "piece of junk" instead. By that time, the lining of the roof was hanging down and I remember driving in my gown praying, "Please, don't let anybody see me get out of this car."

I don't like being the center of attention, but as the bride, that would prove impossible to avoid. As I walked down the aisle, all eyes were upon me – 200 pairs to be exact. "Oh my God, I can't do this," I panicked. "I'm going to throw up."

Our fathers must have been nervous too, because they were as drunk as could be. Neither of them ever drank, but for some reason they decided to share a bottle of Stolichnaya Vodka right before the ceremony. Standing at the altar, Rhonda, my maid of honor, handed my father the bouquet so she could hold up the back of my gown. My father held the flowers and sneaked peeks at my soon-to-be father-in-law, and they were both dying of laughter.

Paul looked over at them and gave them a "What the Hell?" look.

It was hysterical.

Because we were both employed at the Mutual Benefit Insurance Company (I would be starting right after the honeymoon), the Rabbi worked it into his sermon.

He said, "Not only are they employed at Mutual Benefit Life, they are also joined mutually in marriage."

This was too corny even for me!

Being an only child, my parents went all out – the whole nine yards – and spared no expense. There was an open bar, and they hired an orchestra – not a band, not a DJ, an orchestra! When Paul and I walked into the reception room as husband and wife for the first time, all the lights were turned off. The room was filled with pineapples wrapped in gold foil, with a candle sticking out of each of them. 200 lights flickering; it was beautiful.

Later, Viennese tables filled with desserts were wheeled out.

For our honeymoon, we went to an all-inclusive resort, nothing elaborate. I'm not sure if they even had fancy honeymoons back then; you simply did what you could afford.

We stayed at Mt. Erie Lodge in the Poconos, about an hour's drive away. It was one of those places designed for honeymooners with a heart-shaped bathtub in the room. Our favorite thing to do was eat. I have proof because we have tons of photos of us doing just that. Besides eating, we spent lots of time outdoors rowing, swimming, riding bikes, and playing tennis.

After the honeymoon, we rented an apartment in Avenel, New Jersey. We were ready to start life together as a married couple. Even though I loved Paul more than anything, I was having a hard time adjusting to life as a young wife. In a different state with a new job, I became unbelievably homesick. Sometimes I would become a bit hysterical. Undaunted, Paul knew just what to do. Whenever I was feeling blue, he'd tell me to pack my bags. He'd then drive me to Rhode Island for the weekend so I could be with my parents. The fact that he would do anything to make sure I felt happy made me feel like the luckiest girl in the world.

Married Life with Paul

Jersey was not my favorite place in the world, but we would end up living there for almost a decade while Paul worked at achieving what at the time seemed like an impossible dream. Our lives fell into a content – if somewhat predictable– routine, but that would all change in nine and a half years.

There are many fringe benefits to working with your spouse. Besides enjoying our lively conversations during our commute, we felt secure driving into Newark, New Jersey in our twelve-passenger Mutual Benefit Life commuter van. We had many laughs and forged some lasting friendships. Mutual Benefit Life had twenty-one floors. I was on the third, working in customer service. Paul was on the tenth, in the actuarial department.

We would call each other throughout the day and meet in the cafeteria for lunch. Once, we watched another newly-wedded couple in disbelief as they ate their scanty meal, splitting a small salad, sandwich, and drink between them.

"Screw that!" I thought. "Give me onion rings and ice cream!"

We practically needed a fork lift; there was so much food on our plate. It was a wonder we could eat that way and still stay thin.

Paul learned all about the inner workings of the insurance company, but it was the actuaries in his own department who intrigued him. Basically, actuaries determine how long people will live so the life insurance companies can determine their premiums. In addition, they analyze the financial costs of risk and uncertainty using mathematics, statistics, and financial theory. Their work is essential to the insurance industry.

"I could do that. I could be an actuary," he said.

We would soon find out this undertaking was not for the faint of heart. At any given time, there are not many actuaries throughout the country because the process is so rigorous. Paul, who never had to study a day in his life, found himself doing nothing else. It was as if he was training for a marathon. He studied at work (as it was part of the program) and at home, right up until bedtime. He even studied on the weekends.

"This is more difficult than trying to pass the bar," a lawyer friend told him.

Paul never quit, though he came close, lamenting, "I have no life!"

"It's a means to an end," his mother would remind him.

By this time, we had bought a townhouse in Edison, New Jersey where we set up a desk in our unfinished basement. Because Paul hated any noise while studying, we came up with the idea of running the dryer. Not only did the white noise help him concentrate, it drowned out most other sounds as well. Of course, the dryer was empty (most of the time), and our electric bill was outrageous!

One Halloween night, when Paul was downstairs, I laughed and told him I would go outside and sit on a beach chair and hand out candy so the doorbell wouldn't disturb him while he studied.

Some people said, "Boy, what a tyrant."

Others would say, "Wow, what a tough life you have."

To the first, I would reply, "No, he's focused and I do what I can to help him."

To the second, "It is, but we're together. It's not like he's going out and drinking with the guys — he's studying!"

Part of what kept us going was that every time he passed an exam, he received a raise.

We both wanted children, and as we were having trouble conceiving, we decided to find out why. As it turned out, I had endometriosis. I had always been in a tremendous amount of pain during my cycle, but I thought it was par for the course. Unfortunately, even after the recommended surgery, we still didn't conceive. In order to prepare for in-vitro, Paul gave me injections every night.

Because of my heart condition, my obstetrician warned me about possible complications. "If there are multiple fetuses, all but one will have to be aborted."

My cardiologists advised against it altogether, saying pregnancy and labor would put too much of a strain on my heart.

Finally, I saw a specialist in Boston, who informed me, "You're a freight train about to hit a brick wall."

That was when we decided that enough was enough. Pregnancy would be too much of a health risk for me, so I took the specialist's recommendation and had a hysterectomy.

Afterward, I couldn't believe how terrific I felt – no more pain. No more menstrual pain for the rest of my life!

After visiting several agencies, we felt that American adoption wasn't right for us. Our research led us to believe that China would be a better fit. But after finding out that the process could take years and could even fall through at the last minute, we weren't sure we could handle the heartbreak.

"I don't want you to suffer," Paul said to me.

We agreed not to proceed. Although we never had children, we had a fulfilling life and were grateful for all we did have.

"Want to get a dog?" Paul asked me about a year later.

I never owned a dog as a child, but had I known how much joy an animal could bring, I would have gotten one years earlier. Rocco, a white Bichon, was perfect; he was the (furry) child we couldn't have. He was super intelligent, and although he didn't talk, we always knew what he wanted.

I always said he was a human in a vertically challenged body with fur. We named him Rocco because he had a fierce bark. With his name and bark you might expect to see a large, tough dog coming around the corner. Instead, he was a little white dog with black eyes and a black nose to match. His name fit him perfectly, however,

Lucky Twice

because he became our protector, although he never bit anyone.

Our dog groomer came once every three weeks. During one scheduled grooming session, my in-laws were visiting. As soon as the groomer rounded the corner, Rocco recognized her van and ran up the stairs. He took a flying leap into the bed where my father-in-law was still in a sound asleep. Rocco dove and hid under the sheets. It was hysterical.

My parents would dog sit whenever Paul and I went away. He loved my mother and acted like she belonged to him and never wanted my father anywhere near her. Rocco would stare my father down until he got off the couch. Then he would jump up and sit next to her. Sometimes he wasn't satisfied with that. He would give my father dirty looks and bark at him until he left the room. That way he could have her all to himself. If you didn't see it with your own eyes, you wouldn't believe it.

Once, my father accidently opened the front door and Rocco ran out of the house. He immediately gave chase to a skunk and cornered it into the bushes across the street. Not surprisingly, he was sprayed. My father tried his best to pull him away, but Rocco wouldn't back down and was sprayed again. Once Rocco got back into the house, he ran free. It took us months to rid the furniture and Rocco of the skunk smell. I always reminded my

38

father of this story because it happened under his watch.

***

When Paul passed the last of his Actuarial exams, we made plans to go to Washington, D.C. with his parents for his graduation ceremony. When we returned to New Jersey, I decided to throw a party for him to celebrate with his coworkers, friends, and family. We held it at a beautiful hotel, and everyone showed up. What we did not know at the time was that this would turn out to be a farewell party as well, and we would soon leave all of our friends and family in New Jersey.

Mutual Benefit Life was having serious difficulties. They had paid for Paul's education and had given him time to study so he could obtain his degree. Now, because they knew they were about to be taken over by the state, they made us an offer we couldn't refuse. Any employee who left voluntarily would receive a one-and-a-half-year severance package.

Headhunters had already gotten wind of the takeover and were calling Paul from all over the country.

So when Paul heard Mutual Benefit Life's offer, he phoned me from the tenth floor and said, "We're out of here."

I was all for it. My dream was to move back to New England. Because Connecticut was the insurance capital of the world, there was a good possibility of that happening. Sure enough, Connecticut National Life contacted Paul for an interview.

As we waited to hear back, we took a much-needed break to Wildwood, New Jersey. As with most of our vacations, my parents joined us. As close as I was to my mother, I felt Paul was even closer to her. I think they had an extra special relationship because they were so much alike. It was like they came from the same mold.

Our hotel was right on the beach and In the evenings, we had the "Mo and Flo Blues," named after my parents Marvin and Sandy; I recorded every session and still have all the tapes. Paul would play the guitar and make up songs about everything that had transpired during the course of the day. The lyrics were side-splitting, and we were in stitches.

"I've got to go pee," my mother would say, laughing so hard that tears would flow down her cheeks. "I've got to go pee."

The following day, we were all enjoying the beach when Paul went back to the hotel room to find out if he had gotten the job. After hanging up, he opened the patio door and yelled across the beach the amount of money they were offering him to start. It was a lot of money back then, and my parents and I started dancing in celebration. It was so cool.

We now had one week to list our townhouse, pack, and find a place to rent in Connecticut until we built our new house. It was a happy whirlwind. New Jersey had always felt "temporary" to me – "a means to an end" – but moving to Connecticut felt like we were going home.

Traveling

Connecticut was everything I dreamed it would be. It's where we grew roots, built our dream house, and made lifelong friends. From that point forward, the stars seemed to align. Life couldn't be better.

I took the first year off to oversee our new home being built. I handled all the necessary paperwork and learned my way around our new town. Then I landed a great job at a local insurance agency. I worked for several agents and handled the underwriting for life, disability, and long-term care policies. I also worked with the clients to determine if they were medically and financially acceptable for the insurance they were applying for. There were roughly twenty people in the agency, and it was a rewarding place to work and learn. Eventually I went part time, and it was great to have a three-day weekend.

On the weekends, we went to our beach house in Rhode Island. It was a one hour and forty-five-minute drive door to door.

Paul considered it his retreat. Knowing friends would ask to visit, he shook his head and said the answer would be, "No, no, no."

Over time, we did have some friends visit. However, he worked extremely hard and had long hours, so he enjoyed the respite of his quiet, restful weekends.

Paul was always poring over travel books, so it wasn't surprising when he came home with a map of the USA one day.

He said, "Our quest is to visit every state in the country."

When he went on a business trip, he'd mark it on the map with a blue push pin. When I joined him, he used a different color. Always on the go, he'd sometimes return from a business trip, and we'd hop on another flight to a new destination.

Another goal of Paul's was to see all the baseball parks. We would time our vacation around a game. Or if that wasn't possible, he'd set up a backroom tour where we would view the locker rooms, dugouts, bullpens, and broadcasting booth. It was pretty cool. In addition to standing in the stadium, we'd actually go out onto the field.

We never used a travel agent. Paul was in his element as he searched the web making plans and reservations. He did it all. All I had to do was show up.

In the morning as I was getting ready to go to the airport, I'd ask him, "What are we doing today?"

He'd tell me, and off we'd go. It didn't matter to me because we always had fun wherever we went.

Each evening as he planned our itinerary, he would tell me, "We're going to do this, this, and this."

Though he meticulously planned our day, it was never set in stone.

Sometimes, in the mornings, he'd say, "We're going to pull an audible."

It was a football term meaning that we're going to change something — right here and now.

My favorite state, of course, was Hawaii. We flew into Honolulu and took a cruise from there. In the mornings, I would open the window of our balcony and find that we were in a different port. I was glad we did not have to take a helicopter from one island to the next.

Paul's favorite destination was California, simply because it had so much going on. He loved Yosemite National Park. With its towering mountains, granite cliffs, and ancient sequoia trees, it was truly breathtaking.

However, North Dakota was a different story. We felt it was in the middle of nowhere. We did not exactly relish the idea of visiting it anytime soon and kept putting it off. Consequently, it was the last state we'd visited prior to Alaska and Hawaii. We were right; it didn't have much to offer. Bored, we drove along a road with only cornfields to look at. Wanting something for lunch, we stopped at a roadside restaurant in this little town. As we opened the door, every head in the place turned our way. Even though we were dressed in jeans and I wore no jewelry or make-up, they looked at us like we had just committed a crime. We were outsiders, and they knew it. It was the eeriest thing.

But we did it – all the way from California with its crazy traffic to Arizona with the spectacular Grand Canyon. We saw every state and completed our quest!

Never one to stay idle, Paul quickly advanced in the insurance industry, doing everything from disability to life insurance – where he established the rates – and designed annuities. It wasn't until he became an international actuary that he got the chance of a lifetime and began traveling the world over: China, London, Japan, Australia – you name it. First, he would learn the rules and regulations. Then he would make sure that each country's policies complied with the laws of their land. Loving every minute of it, he wanted me to join him. Soon, a map of the world took its place next to the good old USA.

"Quit your job," he said when I turned forty-three, "and travel with me."

"No," I refused. Knowing only a working life, I imagined longs hours of sitting at home with nothing to do between trips.

"Listen," he persisted, "if you don't like it, you'll get another job."

Finally, I agreed.

Not sure that I had made the right decision, I spent my first week crying. In the days that followed, however, I found ways to keep active. For starters, I kept in touch with all my friends and made it a point never to eat lunch alone, meeting up with them during their lunch hour. I joined various organizations and groups — book clubs, piano lessons, volunteering. Paul and I had an agreement that I would handle everything household related — this was no small task since at the time we owned three homes. Under this arrangement, he would not have to do any chores when the weekend came around. All of this, coupled with the fact that I started traveling with Paul, kept my life full and I never did go back to work.

Generally, a limo picked us up and drove us to New York or Boston where most of the flights departed from. We were able to fly first class because of all the points Paul had accumulated throughout the years, but that only slightly eased my dislike of flying.

As our 25th wedding anniversary was fast approaching and Paul had a business trip coming up in London, and we decided to go together. But Paul got called in last minute and had to take an earlier flight. Since it was one of my first international trips, he didn't want me traveling alone. So he arranged for Mike, one of his business partners, to accompany me.

After the limo picked me up, we arrived at Mike's house around four in the morning.

"I'm Paul's replacement," he said. "Happy Anniversary."

My substitute husband took care of my luggage, provided me with company during the long flight, and delivered me safely to my rightful husband who was waiting with a rose.

Paul watched me as I took in London. Later, he told me, "You had a smile from here to there."

In fact, it seemed I had a smile after every first-class flight.

The airline staff came around with champagne and ice cream, asking, "What can we get you?"

"I could get used to being spoiled," I thought.

The hotel was posh. Our room was luxurious but cozy enough to make me feel right at home.

While Paul worked, I meandered through London's bustling streets. I happily took in all the sights, smells, and sounds and explored small shops that sold local handcrafted goods nibbling on crumpets along the way.

When traveling, Paul had an expense account he used for entertaining clients. We never abused it. I would often eat at a McDonald's or some other inexpensive restaurant.

Though I was often out exploring on my own, he did arrange to take some time off once he was finished with business. He took vacation time so we could spend some extra time in each country and go sightseeing together.

When he finished up in London, we took a train into Paris to celebrate our anniversary. It was very different than our Poconos trip twenty-five years earlier, but each was special in their own way.

In other foreign lands, I would take English-speaking tours and often hired a translator. I had just recently discovered sushi when I visited Japan. I wanted to learn how to make it for myself, innocently thinking the fish would be pre-sliced. Obliging, my translator found me an instructor, and I followed her down into a basement filled with Japanese men. There before me was a fish with a sharp knife beside it. I realized that I was expected to chop off its head and tail.

"We're outta here," I informed my translator. I've never de-boned a fish in my life and wasn't about to start now.

My favorite country of all was Spain. Though we did some side trips, we mostly stayed in Barcelona. I fell in love with it, delighted every time I came upon one of the unique structures designed by Antoni Gaudi. They had the effect of making me feel I was in an enchanted land. His imagination seemed to have no boundaries. As I marveled at the magnificent Sagrada Famila cathedral, I felt I stood in the shadows of an architect genius. To this day, it has left a deep impression.

Happiest when exploring new territory, Paul planned three or four major vacations a year. We found it best to leave around major holidays. Since it was generally a crazy time for domestic flights, it was a perfect time to fly out of the country. There was also the added benefit of not having to take extra time off.

As neither one of us came from large families, Thanksgiving wasn't a big deal. Besides, Paul hated turkey. Yet there was no escaping it.

When we were aboard a flight, the staff would inevitably say, "Oh, we have prepared an American Thanksgiving dinner for you."

Amazingly, Paul stepped foot in every country he desired to see – all except one, that is. He always wanted to go to Israel. I admit I held him back a little, but ultimately he decided against it, thinking it was too dangerous at the time.

If it wasn't for Paul, I would have never seen the world. I would have probably been like my parents, just going to the beach in the summer and Cape Cod in the fall. That would've been it.

I'm grateful we lived the life we did before it was too late. Paul lived his dreams. Not too many people can say that.

Cancer Buddies

Paul and my parents hardly ever got sick – until they got cancer, that is.

In 2007, my mother was diagnosed with multiple myeloma, a hematological (blood) cancer typically occurring in the bone marrow. Bone pain, I am told, is one of the worst pains you can ever experience. I know she suffered greatly.

I would drive to Rhode Island in order to be with her at her doctor's appointments and hold her hand while they took fluid out of her hip bone. Through this very painful procedure, she never complained. She just did what she had to do.

The three of us – my father, Paul, and I – would take her to the Dana-Farber Cancer Institute in Boston, Massachusetts. Paul made it a point to be there, researching multiple myeloma extensively; he was the educator of the group and knew all the right questions to ask.

Then in 2009, two years after my mother's diagnosis, Paul was told he had prostate cancer. Our travels now not only included trips to Dana-Farber for my mom, but to the Memorial Sloan

Kettering Cancer Center in New York for Paul, in a desperate attempt to save their lives.

The first course of action for Paul was to have his prostate removed. Most of the time – God willing – the doctors get all the cancerous cells and you are then good for life. At first, this seemed to be the case with Paul. Relieved, we focused on my mother.

Not wanting to face another winter, she told her oncologist, "If I'm going to have treatments, why can't I have them in Florida?"

She was adamant, and he agreed.

A few years earlier, as an investment, Paul and I had purchased a condo in Naples, so we made arrangements for my parents to stay there. Even though she was suffering from the side effects of chemo, she managed to get on a plane with my father. She continued her chemo in Florida and things went on as usual, with us flying down to help out. We even rented a home in Sarasota in the last year of her life so that we could help her more.

In order to monitor his numbers for his Prostate-Specific Antigen (PSA) tests, Paul had blood work done every three months. Two years after his prostate was removed, his PSA numbers – which should have read zero – climbed back up, indicating that the cancer had returned. The next step was radiation – forty-eight rounds of it. At this point, Paul started to work from home. He would go to the hospital every day, and they radiated the area where his prostate used to be, thinking that some of the cancerous cells had escaped. It worked for a while, giving him another two years of being cancer free.

But my mom's health continued to deteriorate. Realizing that her care was beyond us, we hired Fay, a wonderful full-time caregiver. We couldn't have asked for anyone better – she was truly a Godsend – and soon considered her a close friend. She was actually with my father near the end of his life as well.

Things continued to decline for my mother. It got to the point where she was receiving blood transfusion after blood transfusion, each treatment leaving her weaker than before. Sensing that the end was near, my dad asked if we would come stay with them. Taking Rosie, our new dog, with us (Rocco had died from cancer), we stayed at the condo. It was small, but we made it work.

Rosie came into our world a year after we lost Rocco. In the Jewish religion, you name after the dead. Since Rocco was named first, Paul and I were trying to come up with a name for Rosie. We kept thinking of all the names beginning with the letter R, but nothing seemed right for our new puppy.

One day, while Paul was shaving, a Bruce Springsteen song came on the radio. Paul's favorite artist of all time was The Boss. He went to every one of his concerts in New York and New Jersey since he was sixteen and had every album. As a matter of fact, he and his friends would go early to pick up the local paper, the *Star Ledger*, when the ticket forms were published to send in for the future show tickets. Back then, there were no computer or phone sales. First come, first serve, by mail request only. Paul and his friends would buy all the papers, fill out the forms in the parking lot, drive into New York City, and drop the envelopes into the post office nearest the Madison Square Garden, where the concerts were to take place. They always had first-row seats for the performances.

So when a Bruce Springsteen song called "Rosalita" came on the radio, Paul cranked up the volume on the radio and came running to find me.

He said, "Why didn't we think of that?" And Rosalita was born – Rosie for short.

Rosie was a cute-as-a-button Havanese. My mother loved her – maybe not as much as Rocco, but she loved her nonetheless. Rosie knew that she was needed and would snuggle up with her in bed.

Paul would come home from his treatments, utterly exhausted, and find them both in bed. He would join them on the other side. My dad and I would check in on them, fondly calling them the cancer buddies.

Soon after, my mother developed a bloody nose that would simply not stop running, no matter what we did. At the hospital, the doctor told her it was a sign that the multiple myeloma was in its final stages.

"Be honest with me," she said. "How much more time do I have?"

He gave her two to four weeks.

"I want to die at home," was her reply.

We honored her wishes. A hospital bed was delivered, and we put it in the den.

Our condo was on the second floor, and there was no elevator. Some of the men from around the development – close friends of ours – placed her in a chair, carried her up, and got her in bed.

"Debbie, why me?" she said after they left. "Why me?"

It was the first time I had ever heard her complain. "I don't know, Mom. I don't know."

A week later, she began making a crackling noise as she gasped for air.

Concerned, I asked the nurse, "What is this?"

There are symptoms of impending death. Because of her vast experience, the nurse knew what to expect. "It's going to be time soon."

Around lunchtime, everyone was in the kitchen, and I was alone with mom in the den. "Mom, I'm going to have lunch, but I'm right here," I whispered in her ear. "You just rest. We're fine. Don't worry."

The last thing the dying hear is your voice. They can hear right up until the end.

As I walked out, the crackling noise stopped.

I said to the hospice nurse as she walked toward me, "I don't think she's with us anymore."

My Mom died in the month of January, and we flew back from Florida to Rhode Island for the funeral. Her best friend Claire came and played a big role with the funeral planning. My mom met her when they began working at Rhode Island College in the admissions office together in the 1960s. For forty-plus years, every Thursday until my mom grew very sick, they ate lunch together at the same table in the same restaurant. That place

– the Old Canteen in the Historic Federal Hill section in Providence, R.I. – is still in existence and has been since 1956, before I was even born. It never changed with its pink painted walls and white linen table cloths. Claire suggested that it was only fitting to have the luncheon after the cemetery at the Old Canteen, and that's exactly what we did, inviting everyone there for lunch in memory of my mom.

After her funeral, my father decided to stay in Naples and we went back home with him to Florida.

But Paul's numbers started going up again. This time, he was prescribed hormonal therapy and received monthly shots to suppress his testosterone. For a while, the cancer was under control.

Then it reared its ugly head again.

Out of options, the doctors from Sloan Kettering told him, "You need to start chemo."

It was at this point Paul decided to leave his beloved job, the one he had worked so hard for, and went on disability.

Like my mother before him, he declared, "If I have to do chemo, I want to do it in Florida."

He wanted to stay in Naples, but we brought him back to our rental home in Sarasota. It was very difficult on all of us, but especially Dad. So, we moved back to the condo in Naples with Dad full-time while our new home was built.

From then on, Paul was either getting chemo or was exhausted from it and spent most of his time on our lanai enjoying the balmy weather while listening to music. He also liked playing Sudoku – he liked the challenging ones – or following the Mets on a special baseball app. He was as happy as could be expected. Through it all, there was not one day he didn't make me laugh. Paul had an incredible sense of humor. He always dressed conservatively until the last year of his life, when he started to buy the most outrageous clothes he could find. Even though they were as loud as could be, he was never embarrassed to be seen wearing them.

We were a very private family. Other than our closest friends, most people never knew my mother and Paul had been fighting cancer. We didn't want to be bothered with people calling us all the time and asking for details. We were living it. Why would we want to sit on the phone going over all the symptoms, comments, or suggestions? People meant well, but almost everyone has had some crisis in their life. We wanted to laugh every day, not have to live it over and over again on the phone.

***

"I think I've pulled a muscle in my neck," Paul said one day as he made an appointment with a physical therapist.

The therapist confirmed his self-diagnosis. They took some tests, arranged for an x-ray, and set up his first session. When we went for his first physical therapy appointment, the therapist excused herself to view the x-ray and test results. We knew something was wrong when she returned. We watched as her face turned pure white.

"I'll tell you what," she said. "I'm more than happy to treat you, but not until after you speak to your doctor."

She knew. I imagine she had gotten the blood results back.

We visited the oncologist that afternoon. I instantly knew what the diagnosis was going to be. Based on his expression, Paul did too. Although my Mom had a different type of cancer, he was experiencing the same type of bone pain. And once the cancer gets into the bones, it's often the beginning of the end. This was the case for both my mother and Paul.

We learned more than we ever thought we needed to know about cancer, but after exploring all avenues and visiting many of the best oncologists in the world, we knew there was truly no more help.

I didn't want to lose my mom or Paul, but they had suffered for too many years. Both had been so strong and never complained. The last thing I did for them was to let them die with dignity. Toward the end of their lives, I believed it would be selfish of me to continue to keep them alive and in pain. What for? Another week? Another month?

"Debbie, I want to go into the hospice down the street," Paul said when he found out he only had a week to live. "I don't want to die in the house like your mom. I don't want you to have those memories."

When you start a life with someone, you imagine growing old together.

My dad always said, "The good die young."

I know it to be true because on August 12, 2016, at the age of fifty-six, Paul lost his battle. And we lost a good, good guy.

Numb, I found myself once again flying back to Rhode Island with my father to bury another loved one. I was astonished at the number of friends, family, and co-workers who came from New Jersey and Connecticut to attend Paul's funeral.

I kept thinking to myself, "I wish he could be here to see how much everyone loved and respected him."

After the graveside service, I invited everyone to a restaurant for lunch before they traveled back to their respective states. When I asked if anyone wanted to share a funny story about Paul, they all had one to tell. One of his co-workers told a story about Paul's backpack. Like most executives, Paul carried a briefcase early on in his career, but he soon traded it in for a blue backpack. He kept everything but the kitchen sink in it. If you needed anything, it was in that backpack. Not one person at the funeral failed to mention it. I ended up keeping it and can't imagine getting rid of it.

Another funny story is that when Paul traveled to another country, everyone knew that they had to find him an ice cream shop. He had to have his ice cream fix every night. Paul never drank liquor, but ice cream was a necessity.

In this time of grief, I was able to laugh and realized Paul could make me smile even in death. I knew he was laughing with us.

Father's Illness

Back in the sixties, when I was growing up in Cranston, there was a Swiss-owned pharmaceutical company just two streets over. Everyone in the neighborhood complained about the horrible stench it omitted. Every once in a while, officials would shut it down pending an investigation. Inevitably, the stench would start up again. I remember that it was particularly bad in the summers, when we had the windows open.

Later, it was discovered that they were dumping toxic chemicals into the water. Not only was the water contaminated, but so was our soil, since the water seeped into it. This chemical plant was poisoning everything around us, from the air we breathed, to the water we drank, to the food we planted. It wasn't until I was twelve that they finally closed the plant down for good.

My mother and our neighbor died from multiple myeloma. When my father was also diagnosed with multiple myeloma, I believed that there had to be a connection. I began calling neighbors and reached out to other Cranston residents.

Soon, people began to respond, telling me who they had lost. Not all the deaths were caused by multiple myeloma, but there were enough cases of cancers and other diseases to be considered a cluster.

I personally know of three women who grew up on my street and were infertile like me. The plant is still there; they can't tear it down for fear it would unearth more chemicals.

Did my parents get cancer because they lived next to this plant? I think so, but there was nothing I could do about it, not when I was about to lose my father. Besides being possibly exposed to these chemicals for years, there is no denying that losing his wife and then Paul took a toll on him.

The four of us had been so close in life. Our time together was filled with joy and laughter. In fact, we were always laughing. My father didn't want all that joy to end. Years earlier, before they got sick, he took measures to make sure we would be together in death too.

"C'mon Deb," my dad said one day. "We're going to buy plots."

Paul and I had previously discussed our funeral agreements, and he always said he would prefer to be cremated. I hardly ever put my foot down, but I told him that was not an option because I wanted us to be buried together. He said if that was the case, he wanted to be buried in Rhode Island because Narragansett Beach was his favorite place. Even so, Paul and my mother refused to join my father in his "morbid" shopping trip.

"If they can't do it," my father, the tough one of the group said, "we have to do it."

Although I thought it was kind of superstitious, I went along so he wouldn't have to do it alone.

First, we found a cemetery in Rhode Island, and then a grassy spot for our plots. We even decided who would be in which one. My dad was the one closest to the outside road; that way he could order Chinese food if he wanted take-out. My mother's and mine were in the middle, with Paul's on the other side because my father felt the men should be on the outside, protecting the women.

"Don't you want to see what we picked out?" I asked Paul.

"No," was his firm answer.

I understood. It certainly was eerie seeing my name and date of birth already on my tombstone. Of course, Paul would end up seeing them when my mother passed away.

Now, I knew I would soon be burying yet another loved one in Swan Point cemetery.

But my father had an extra burden. He knew that when he was gone, the three of them would be together and I would be left alone.

"Listen. I love your daughter," Allen reassured him. "I promise you, I will take care of her."

A very suspicious man, my father didn't know what to make of this. "Come on, he just met you," he said when we were alone.

"Dad, he's very good to me," I said, finally convincing him. Besides, I had a great track record, already having chosen Paul.

Hospice was with my Dad during the last week of his life. I was with him as much as possible too, but I had to keep my cardiologist appointment.

As soon as Allen and I left the doctor's office, I turned my cell phone back on and listened to the voicemail message the hospice nurse had left. She told me my father would probably die within the hour.

Thank God we made it back in time; it was as if my dad waited for me.

"I'm here," I told him as he made that cracking sound I knew oh so well. "Don't worry; I'm going to be alright." I let him know he could rest, that I would be okay, and not to worry.

At the age of eighty-five, my dad died peacefully in his apartment, confident that I had another good man by my side.

I was with my mother, my husband, and now my father to the very end. They did not die alone. Because I lost all three of them in such a short time, it had left me with no time to mourn. I had been so strong for so long, but now it was time for me to grieve. The truly amazing thing is that I didn't have to do it alone.

Once again, I found myself flying back to Rhode Island for yet another funeral, but this time I had Allen by my side. We had only been together for two months, but he had no intention of letting me go alone. Allen stayed at the hotel, respecting my wishes not to attend the funeral. I felt it was not the appropriate time to introduce him to my family and friends. However, he took me to the funeral home early in the morning so we could view my father before they closed the casket.

Matters of the Heart

It seems that in the midst of taking care of my family, I had forgotten to take care of myself.

Throughout their illnesses, I lived in five different houses, four of which I had to clean out and put on the market. I sorted through every closet, drawer, and box, deciding what to keep and what to give away. There I was, loading everything into black trash bags and throwing them down the stairs. Though it was nice to have something to occupy my mind during this time of turbulence, I was going against my cardiologist's direct orders.

When I was twenty-one, I was diagnosed with Marfan's Syndrome, a condition affecting the connective tissues – heart, eyes, blood vessels, and skeleton. It can become life-threatening if your aorta – the large blood vessel that carries blood from your heart to the rest of your body – thickens.

My doctor explained it to me this way: your aorta root keeps stretching like a rubber band that loses elasticity. If it expands too much, you will have an aneurysm. Some historians believe that Abraham Lincoln had Marfan's Syndrome. While this was never proven, he had many of its characteristics. People who have it tend to be tall and lanky – like basketball players — with disproportionately long limbs and fingers. Often when you hear of a young athlete dropping dead on the court, it is because, unbeknownst to them, they have the syndrome. With improved recognition, monitoring, and treatment, such occurrences are fortunately rare.

At first, my yearly echocardiogram revealed that my aortic valve was getting bigger. It eventually stabilized, leaving me with the impression that if I made it this far, I was home free. Besides, I had always been careful and followed my cardiologist's advice by avoiding rigorous sports and not lifting anything heavy...well, up until then that is. Getting ready to move requires a lot of heavy lifting. And with my family ill (Allen wasn't in the picture yet), I felt as though I was the only one who could do it.

According to the Social Readjustment Rating Scale developed by psychiatrists Thomas Holmes and Richard Rahe, the death of a spouse has a value of 100 points on the scale measuring stress. When you factor in the death of my parents and moving, my score was off the charts. All of this stress wasn't adding up for a healthy heart and when I went for my yearly checkup, my test results proved it.

"What are you doing here?" exclaimed a young doctor in Naples, looking at my echocardiogram results. "If you were my relative, I'd tell them you need to get the surgery now! Not tomorrow, now!"

"Ah, the hell with him," I thought defiantly. "He doesn't know my history."

Yet his diagnosis rattled me, so I called my doctor in Connecticut. Since I had been under his care for twenty years, I just wanted to be sure.

"You're fine. I know it's getting large, but you're not at risk," he said.

However, since he hadn't reviewed my case in several years, he asked me to send him the most recent medical records.

When Allen came into my life, he accompanied me for a follow-up appointment in May.

"So, how are you feeling after surgery?" asked the young cardiologist.

"I didn't go yet."

"Are you kidding me?" he yelled.

Allen and I were determined to find the best surgeon in the country, feeling that money should be no object when it came to our health. There are only four doctors in the country who can perform this operation. We researched and interviewed the doctors in Philadelphia, New York, and Cleveland over the phone.

We hopped in the car when we decided to meet the surgeon in Philadelphia – besides having a great bedside manner, his staff was outstanding. The University of Pennsylvania hospital was state of the art. It also didn't hurt that he had already performed hundreds of aorta valve surgeries and thousands of open-heart operations as well, never losing a patient.

Two weeks later, I was on the operating table.

"Mr. Seaman, you've got to see this," the doctor told Allen after surgery. "I took a picture of your wife's valve. It's one of the worst cases I've ever seen in all my years of medicine. Give me your cell phone number and I'll send you a photo." Within a few minutes, we both had the picture on our phones and the doctor described what we were looking at.

It showed five holes where the blood was leaking out of my valves. Arteries should not be more than an inch wide; mine were three to four inches and ready to burst.

I knew I was lucky when I was told, "If you didn't have the surgery, you wouldn't be with us in three weeks." I felt luckier still when I heard my surgeon would be leaving for South America on Monday and then to Europe for several months to teach other surgeons this intricate surgery.

When Allen saw me laying there, hooked up to all sorts of tubes and bags of fluids, he told me how brave I was. But the truth of the matter was that I would not have gotten the surgery if Allen had not been in the picture. I would have done nothing and died of an aneurysm.

Allen kept the picture of my valve that the doctor had texted, so I guess you can say he now carries a piece of my heart around. At any rate, he will always have my heart, and I will always have his.

How many people do you know who would stay by your side after only three months? Allen was there for me through my dad's death, accompanied me to Rhode Island so I could attend the funeral, and six months later he drove me to Philadelphia, and was now taking care of me after my heart surgery.

Death and illness are just a part of life, and I have been reminded of that all too often. It was certainly a sad day when my dog Rosie passed away. It is one of the tragedies of owning a pet – you grow attached, but then you have to say goodbye.

Rosie was happy and playful until suddenly she started sleeping more and more. This was concerning because she was only around seven, and her breed generally lives to be fifteen.

Because we were going away for the 4th of July, we hired a mother and daughter team to dog sit for us. When we came home, Rosie was a little distraught. This was to be expected because we were away for five days, but otherwise she seemed fine. Later, as we were playing with her, she vomited. We weren't too concerned at first because we thought the sitters had let her eat grass or something. We thought she'd soon be better. But not long after, she was unable to stand up.

"Something's wrong," I told Allen. "We'd better take her to the vet."

Next thing you know, they're doing all sorts of tests on Rosie at the clinic.

"Why don't you go out?" the vet said. "When you come back, I'll give you a full report."

This walk helped clear my mind and face the facts – the end was near for Rosie.

"It's not good," the vet told us when we returned. "She has intestinal cancer."

It was hard news to accept, especially since we had recently buried so many family members.

"We could keep her alive for a while," she went on, "by giving her chemo."

"No way," I said. "I'm not putting Rosie through that. We'll put her to sleep, but first I want to spend some time with her."

Allen and I sat on the floor, and I held Rosie in my lap.

"What's next?" I thought on this sad day. It made me appreciate Allen more than ever. I told him, "You're the only one I have left."

That night, we had Rosie cremated. We placed her alongside Rocco in his urn. I had given Allen instructions that if my health ever failed, I wanted their urns in my casket. That is how much they meant to me. They were there for me through many tough times. I still think about them to this day. If a dog commercial comes on TV, it sets my heart aflutter. We might not get another dog anytime soon, but those memories are always near and dear to me. When we first met, Allen had told me he wasn't a dog person. He wouldn't walk or clean up after Rosie, but over time, he sure did warm up to her and came to love her as much as I did. The fact that he was there with me when Rosie died meant everything. Allen cried just as much as me when Rosie was put to rest, if not more.

Allen's Story

Growing Up

I was the baby of five, born on April 30, 1959, at Saint Mary's Hospital in Passaic, New Jersey. My brother, Jimmy, was eighteen years my senior. I really looked up to him, both figuratively and literally.

My home life was the typical "scared-of-the-parents" deal that was characteristic of the era. They told us what to do, and we obeyed without question. Back then, we played outside, but when the streetlights came on, you had better get home or else Daddy would hunt you down. If you were lucky, he would just yell at you; if not, you might get a good smack across the ass. That kept most of us in line, but once when my brother was acting like a complete idiot, my father threw him into the wall. I swear to God, to this day, the lights in that room don't work right. My brother never acted like an ass again – well, at least not around my father.

We had a lot of great times though: snowmobiling, hunting, fishing, playing horseshoes, baseball, and tennis. You name it, and we were outdoors doing it.

Maybe all that fresh air spoiled me, because from day one I hated school. It bored me to death, but I still managed to ace through all my classes even though I never paid attention or even studied. In grammar school, I was the wise guy who loved the girls. I was always getting in trouble for teasing them. Their mothers would call up my mother to complain. One teacher even slammed me against the wall when he caught me bothering a girl.

"What's the matter with you, you stupid bastard?" he hollered at me.

One thing I was really good at was chess. My teacher, John, was a great guy. He had a six by six-foot chessboard on the wall so that students could learn to play. I watched a couple of games and picked it up right away. From then on during my lunch period, I played chess with John almost every day. I don't think he ever beat me.

"Get the fuck out of here," he'd say when he lost, flinging the board across the room.

Word got around. Soon kids began stopping by, hoping to see him blow up and send chess pieces flying to the farthest corners. All of this didn't stop him from wanting to help me out though. Far from it.

When I was twelve years old, he wanted me to find out where I ranked in the state.

I was thinking that my mother and father didn't have money for that, but John wouldn't understand. So I just said, "Nah, I don't want to do it."

As I got older, I started to take school a little bit more seriously. My parents' education was limited; my father only had a fourth-grade education and my mother a ninth.

It wasn't like I could bring home a book and say, "Ma, could you help me with this?"

There was none of that, but I did ask her a couple of times.

Her standard reply was, "I don't know," or "Maybe if we tried this."

To which I would say, "Oh, Ma. Even I know that ain't right."

After that, I more or less paid attention in school.

My school was divided up just like our town: half Polish and half Italian. The Italians had the money; the Pollocks were the hard workers. I was Polish, and the teachers were mostly Italians. I'm a big guy, but there were guys half my size playing football because their daddy was an elected official. I could not believe it. I don't go for those political games now, and I didn't go for them as a kid. I didn't like the favoritism. If a teacher liked a kid because his parents were somebody in town or he was a brownnoser, I saw right through it.

***

My grandfather built a home on Mets Lake, New York when he was only in his twenties. Then, in the 1950s, my parents purchased a little country bungalow nearby. In the 1990s, Janice and I bought my grandfather's home and one of the neighbor's houses. My sister, Judi, and her husband bought one as well. You could say that it became a family tradition. I had been going to Mets Lake my entire life.

In 1974, when I was fifteen, we were staying at the Bungalow when my father said to me, "I'll wake you up early in the morning. We'll go fishing, just you and me."

He never woke me up.

"He's sleeping like a baby; leave him alone," he said to my mother. "I'll go by myself, and if he wants, I'll take him fishing tonight."

He never came home. We soon learned he fell out of the boat and drowned.

"Get up, get up," one of my aunts ran into the house screaming. "Your father's dead!"

That's how I woke up. It was horrific. In a state of shock, my siblings and I got out of bed, threw some clothes on, and washed our faces. I was still in disbelief as the state police walked over the property and a clergyman visited while neighbors brought us food. All I could think about was how my dad had asked me to go with him. I carried that guilt around for years. I still think about it sometimes.

My father's death left me numb. Afterward I just went through the motions. My attitude in high school was, "Who cares?"

"Want to play sports?"

"Nah."

"You want to do this?"

"Nah."

But I did have one highlight. One Saturday, I went over to Garfield High School to watch a football game. I was standing by the fence near one of the end zones, waiting for my friends to show up. All of a sudden, this guy walks up and starts talking to me about the game. He had a big hat on and was dressed like he was going to be in a John Wayne cowboy movie with a deerskin jacket and matching boots up to his knees – the kind where you tie a million knots all the way up to the top.

We talked a little. I was thinking, "Wow, I just met Eddie Brigati. The Eddie Brigati from the musical group The Young Rascals."

I didn't know it then, but he would become a huge influence in my life. He and I would also become family when I married Janice, his cousin. Hands down, he's one of the best friends I've ever had.

While working at Chester Pharmaceuticals after high school, I enrolled at Fairleigh Dickinson, where I maintained a 3.6 GPA.

My Wyckoff neighbor came running over to my house one day and said, "You know you're a summa cum laude?"

"How do you know?"

"It's in the newspaper," she said, handing me the article.

Pretty good for a guy who never read a book in his life. Although, I did read a book when I was twenty-five. It was about a boating accident; maybe it hit too close to home because I never read another book.

Meeting Janice

When I was a volunteer fireman in Garfield, New Jersey, a fellow fireman wanted to set me up on a blind date with his neighbor, Janice. He and his wife thought that we would be perfect together. As it turns out, they were right, but first I would have to pass muster with Janice's family.

A few days later, while running a fundraiser for the firehouse, I noticed a small cluster of women huddled together, giving me sideway glances. They asked me all sorts of questions and then would whisper among themselves.

Well, I must have gotten their stamp of approval, because I got to meet Janice shortly afterward. Two years older than me, she was a business-minded, take-no-prisoners kind of girl. And I liked what I saw: she was casually dressed with a nice, sharp look about her. Cool, good looking, streetwise, and smart, she had it all. I'm 6'2" and Janice was 5'2", but somehow she seemed taller — a fireball of energy. Her presence was just amazing. From the way she sat to her quick wit, she caught my eye. I could tell she was going places. She was working for the Meadowlands, the biggest racetrack at the time. Eventually she would work her way up from secretary to be the first female chief inspector for the New Jersey Racing Commission.

"Wow, this girl has got something," I thought.

We began talking every night.

Janice finally asked me, "You want to go on a date?"

When I picked her up, she informed me, "I have to take a ride down to the Shore. I have to pick something up at my friend's and then drop it off at my house in Forked River."

"Okay, cool," I said. "I'll go with you."

When we got there, I met her friend Linda and Linda's husband, Gary. It turned out that the "something" we had to pick up was a clothes dryer.

"Come on," Gary said. "It's in the garage."

I backed the car up to where he was pointing, but when I turned around, Gary was nowhere in sight. I had to pick up this freaking dryer, put it in the trunk, and tie it down by myself.

I think he was taking advantage of me because it was our first date. Maybe he thought Janice and I weren't going to last.

"Screw it," he was probably thinking. "Let him do all the work. She's getting the dryer for free."

As we drove to Forked River, Janice and I were having a great time laughing and talking. When we got there, I carried the dryer into her house. After completing this Herculean task, we went out to dinner.

Overall it was a fantastic date, but Janice was hesitant about going out with me again because she knew I liked to party. Here I was, a big dude in my early twenties sowing his wild oats. But I was willing to change my ways for her. She meant that much to me, and we started seeing each other a couple of times a week.

A few months later, in November, Janice was turning twenty-five and her sisters were planning a surprise party for her. They invited forty guests and told me to bring my mother so she could meet the family. At the party, I noticed everybody was saying hello to this guy they called Cousin Eddie. I didn't give it a second thought as I was making sure my mother was comfortable.

A couple of weeks later, Janice said, "You want to go by Eddie's?"

"Why? You mean your cousin Eddie?"

"You know who Eddie is, right?"

I'm like, "Oh, yeah, yeah."

I had no clue. It turned out that he was Eddie Brigati, the Young Rascals star I had met twelve years earlier at the football stadium.

Cousin Eddie treated me like a brother, but some of Janice's other relatives weren't quite so welcoming.

When I had my first Thanksgiving with her family a few weeks later, one of them said to me, "Oh, you're one of them."

"I guess so," I said. "What does that mean?"

"You're not Italian, so you're not one of us. You don't belong here."

"I don't belong here," I told Janice. "I guess it's my last Thanksgiving."

"That's right," she said. "The way they treated you, you don't have to go anymore."

From then on, I just picked which family gatherings to attend.

Janice knew I loved horses and going to the racetrack because my brother Jimmy used to take me when I was a little kid. I often accompanied her to the Meadowlands. It was always exciting. She was good at what she did and got to meet the likes of George Steinbrenner, the owner of the New York Yankees, and actors Don Ameche and Burt Reynolds, to name a few. Then there were the baseball players, including Roy White, who would stop by her office. Janice knew everybody. It was just amazing.

One day, when we were walking toward the grandstand, I saw all these young, beautiful women hanging around this guy wearing a pair of cowboy boots and a Stetson hat. He's walking around with this entourage when all of a sudden, he greeted Janice, "Hey Jan. Hey, how you doing?"

"He's a multibillionaire," Janice informed me later. "He asked me out to dinner once. Even though he's worth eight billion dollars, he's a real nice down-to-earth guy."

"Wait a minute," I said. "He asked you to go out, and you're dating me?" Now, I'm thinking something's wrong with this picture. I would have married this guy for that amount of money. "Why the hell are you going out with me?"

"I don't know yet," she said with a smile.

All joking aside, we were the best of friends. It meant a lot to have somebody I could trust, somebody I could have fun with, somebody I wanted to spend the rest of my life with. That was my Janice.

Wedding & Honeymoon

We followed the old Italian-American "rules" of dating: one year of getting to know each other, followed by a yearlong engagement. Then when I asked Janice to marry me, she was like, "What have you been waiting for?"

My father-in-law and I got along famously, always busting each other's chops, so it was no different when I asked permission for his daughter's hand in marriage.

"Hey Pops," I said one day. "I have an idea."

"What's that?"

"You know, why don't I just buy the cow instead of getting the milk for free?"

He looked at me and said, "You son-of-a-bitch. Yeah you could."

Even though I was laughing on the outside, I was feeling quite shy on the inside.

Janice's family, forever protective of her, were not pleased with how I stated my intentions, but they knew they were honorable. When Janice and I were dating, I would walk through blizzards, a mile from my house to hers, in order to dig her car out and shovel the family's sidewalk.

"If he's doing this for you, he's got to love you," Janice's father said to her. "Or else he's nuts. It's one or the other."

We had a beautiful wedding with almost all of our family attending from both sides. A violin player walked among the tables at our reception, but one of the most important things for me was to make sure my mother was treated like a queen for the day.

"Ma," I said. "If there's anything you want, anything at all, you just come and see me." Then I told her, "There's this lady over there named Fran. Go to her, she's in charge and will get you whatever you want. If she doesn't satisfy you, come back to your son."

She looked at me and said, "Who are you all of a sudden?"

My mother was the type to say at cocktail hour, "You know, I could go for a piece of cake and a cup of coffee." So if we were having prime rib at the reception and she wanted a hotdog, I wanted her to have it. I even danced the polka with her. It was hysterical, and everybody clapped when we were done. We had a great time.

Of course, I was the typical man and got pretty drunk. When it was all over, Janice had to drive us home. The following day, we left for our honeymoon. We spent four days in the Poconos, followed by four days in the Catskills, and finally four days in Atlantic City.

The only problem was that I had a horrible hangover and wound up taking a long nap as Janice drove us. When I woke up, we were in the Catskills and not the Poconos.

"Honey," I said, "you're like fifty, sixty miles off. All you had to do was take Route 80."

"Well, you had to get drunk? This is all your fault."

"Okay, okay, let's just turn around and go back."

Though she never let me live this down, we hardly ever fought during our twenty-nine years of marriage.

When we arrived at the resort, we got ready for dinner in our suite, which had a heart-shaped tub. Dressed to impress in a black suit with a red tie and hankie, I looked really sharp. Total Al Capone swag.

As I mentioned before, I'm a pretty decent-sized guy, so when our server gave me a one-inch by one-inch piece of cake, I looked at him and pointed to my plate. "Do I look like a fucking bird to you? Where's the rest of my dessert?"

A hush fell over the restaurant.

"That's all you're entitled to," he said in a pompous voice.

"Get the fuck outta here."

I thought it was supposed to be an all-you-can-eat buffet.

The rest of our honeymoon went according to plan. We had a wonderful time, but it couldn't last forever. So we returned home to the house we bought in Wyckoff, New Jersey and went back to work.

The Routines of Marriage

Our marriage was smooth and easy. We'd often arrive home around the same time, but if one of us got back earlier, we'd start cooking so the other could relax when they got home.

If Janice cleaned the kitchen, then I would clean the bathrooms. Everything flowed because we worked as a team. I mean, it was just wonderful – like we could read each other's minds. Plus, she was a Betty Crocker homemaker; she cooked, cleaned, and even did a little bit of sewing. She was the perfect woman in every way. And with her great sense of humor, we never had a dull moment in our lives.

Ever full of energy, she would take on part-time jobs in addition to her full-time job. She even found a way to work during her lunch hour. There was a market research company right near the racetrack, so she would go there and have lunch.

"Oh, and by the way," she would tell me, "they paid me $150."

After about a year or two of marriage, we unsuccessfully tried to conceive. We visited in-vitro specialists and found out Janice wasn't able to carry her own child. At that point, we considered getting a surrogate.

After thinking about it, Janice concluded, "Genetically it wouldn't be my baby, but it will always be yours."

That made her uncomfortable because she figured I could always say something like, "Hey, don't talk to my kid like that."

So we decided to let nature take its course. If we had a child …wonderful. If not, we still had each other. We went with it and never conceived. She then began to worry I was going to leave her.

"Listen," I'd say. "I married you for you. I didn't know if we were going to have kids or not. I want you; you're always going to be first in my life."

"Really? Are you sure?"

"Honey," I said, "it's about me and you. Our wedding song was 'Just You and I,' there's nobody else in that song."

Since we had no children, we didn't have to cook. Eating out once or twice a day was no big deal. We'd go out, try somewhere new, and maybe take some friends or family with us. Or if we were eating at home, we'd say to our family and friends,

"Come on over. We'll go get some pizza or ribs or have a nice little barbecue."

Though we were always having parties and people over, we guarded our alone time carefully.

When we went on vacations and a friend would say, "Hey, come on, we'll all go together," we'd decline. Or, "Come by our house and stay for the weekend." We wouldn't do that either, no. We'd go, but we'd stay at a hotel so we could come and go as we please. The one thing we didn't want in our lives was aggravation. You know the old saying, "You can pick your friends, but you can't pick your family?"

One exception to that old saying was our Cousin Eddie; we'd often take vacations together and didn't let a week go by without seeing him. He was the absolute greatest. Besides being married to Janice (and later Debbie), being friends with Eddie Brigati was the highlight of my life.

I went from that horrible moment when I lost my dad, wishing I could have been there to save him, to having a guy like Eddie come in my life. He really made the quality of our lives much better. I got to meet people, visit places, and experience things I would never have had the chance to do without him.

Eddie would say something like, "I've got to go to a dinner in New York. Want to come?"

"Sure, why not?"

Janice and I would jump into his car with him and Susan and head off to a function where there could be over 300 people. Many of them would come up to Eddie like he was God.

He'd introduce us, saying, "This is my cuz."

We would sheepishly tell them, "Yeah. We're cousins."

It was really cool. Eddie opened up my life to a lot of things. I got to meet people like Tommy James, Micky Dolenz of the Monkees, Tony Orlando, Johnny Farina of Santo and Johnny, and Joey Dee and the Starliters.

One time, Janice and I went to a Tony Orlando show in Vegas.

"Hey, Tony," I screamed out from the audience. I don't care about anything. After all, I'm from Jersey. "My cousin says hi."

He stopped the show and asked, "Who's your cousin?"

"Eddie Brigati."

"Don't leave. After the show, you're coming backstage."

Backstage, we took pictures with Tony, and I called Eddie. We all started singing "Groovin'" to him over the phone. It was quite a moment. Singing to Eddie with Janice and Tony Orlando was such a thrill. It was like, "Wow!"

About two years before Janice passed away, Eddie called up one day. "I'm in Saint Augustine. I want to come over and ask you guys something."

"Alright, come on down."

"Susan and I are getting married," he told us when he arrived. "Would you be my best man?"

Here he was – Rock and Roll Hall of Famer, Music Writer Hall of Famer, gold records, and fame. He knows millions of people.

I'm thinking, "Rich people, famous people, and here he is asking me to be his best man? Something's wrong with this picture."

"He knows all these celebrities, up the wazoo," I said to Janice. "All these rich, rich people. And he's picking me?"

"I told you," she said. "Eddie always liked you."

"Yeah, but best man for Eddie? That's going in my obituary."

For me to be his best man, I was very humbled.

Janice and I went shopping with Eddie and Susan to buy shirts and shorts that matched. We were laughing because Eddie's like 5'5" and I'm 6'2", Susan's around 5'7", but Janice – the matron of honor – was 5'2." We thought it was funny that Susan and I were closer in height, while Janice and Eddie were around the same size.

The wedding took place on a beach in St. Augustine, and the reception that followed was at an exclusive luxury hotel.

"Wow," I thought as I stood next to Eddie during the ceremony. "Look at where this went. I was twelve years old standing at a fence when I met him, and today I'm his best man."

Working & Inventing

I started out as a pharmaceutical production operator in 1982 for Chester, a manufacturing site in Nutley, New Jersey that developed pharmaceutical products. Not long after being hired, I was promoted to overseeing the quality improvement department. Seeing my potential, my manager talked me into going back to school, where I majored in Business Management. It was a perfect fit, as I was good at teaching and pinpointing employees' strengths.

Figuring that allowing me to advance was cheaper than hiring an engineer, I was promoted to manufacturing where I was in charge of new products. I was good at what I did and eventually created my own niche.

My boss would give me an assignment, telling me, "I want you to save us $700,000 a year on manufacturing this product. We'll give you six months."

I did it in two months. "Alright," I said. "What's next?"

Impressed, and I think a little jealous, he said, "We've got a brand-new plant down in South

Carolina. Why don't you relocate and work there?"

"My wife's not going to leave her job at Meadowlands so we can move to the boonies," I said. "There ain't no way that's going to happen."

Pissed because I wouldn't do what he wanted, he set out to make my life miserable.

Chester had developed an effective diet product but couldn't figure out how to manufacture it in bulk. In order to find a solution, scientists from our headquarters in Basel, Switzerland flew in to meet with our engineers, a few supervisors, and me. The meeting was proving unproductive.

To this day, I don't remember exactly what I said to the scientist sitting next to me, but I suggested, "Why don't we try this? Because if we could do this, it should change that."

Whatever I said to him worked. I received thank you letters from the Switzerland scientists with a little bonus inside. One even wanted to put me on the patent, but my boss knocked that idea down. This was a huge disappointment because I would have been set for life.

Perturbed, I decided to leave and walked out on them. I just couldn't take it anymore. People couldn't believe that I had the balls to do it, but I was prepared.

My wife had a startup business in the works. The idea for Janice's business came about one night when we were at a restaurant and noticed two rednecks who had just gotten married. The groom was trying to eat crab legs, when some of it squirted out and landed all over his wife's wedding gown.

"There's got to be a better way," I thought, watching them.

The next evening, Janice and I designed a prototype: a pair of scissors with a splatter guard where you could insert the blade into the open end of the crab leg. It made cutting easy and relatively mess free. We got it patented and our business, Sea Scissors, was born.

We traveled all over the country to find the best manufacturer and chose one in Indiana. From there we started to sell them. However, to save money, we would later use a company in China.

Janice's next inspiration came when we were out fishing with Linda and Gary. They would come down to visit us in Florida but didn't like holding their reels as they waited for the fish to bite. So, Janice took one of the cup holders and designed it to hold the fishing pole, making it possible to fish hands-free.

Then all of a sudden, Janice got a letter from Bloomingdale's. It read, "We would like to sell your Sea Scissors, but we need two more products in your seafood line before offering it to our customers."

Janice got right to work and created the Sea Shucker.

When eating oysters or clams, you need a knife to pry the shell open and a shucker to scoop the meat out. So, she combined them. Hey, it wasn't like it was brain surgery.

For our third product, Janice designed a scissor for cleaning shrimp. It had a little hook on the end to remove the veins, and we added ridges on the inside of the handles for removing the tail. Then you pull the black stuff out with the little hook on the end. Bloomingdale's took us on, and we wound up selling thousands of our merchandise. The Sea Scissors even won best seafood gadget from *Bon Appétit* magazine one year.

From there, we got in other stores like LL Bean, Sur la Table, Home Goods, and Bed, Bath, and Beyond. When we told family and friends, they could hardly believe it. Janice was a big star — it really was something to walk in these stores and see the products there for the first time.

The amazing thing was that we never paid a dollar's worth for public relations. We were featured in gourmet cooking magazines and newspapers across the country.

One article was featured in the *Bergen Record* with Janice's picture. The caption read: "Edward Scissorhands has nothing on this girl."

When she was interviewed by Table Talk, a weekly column by a local food professional Bev Mortenson, Janice was asked, "What is your most memorable food experience?"

She replied, "It was New Year's Eve 2000. We prepared an outstanding dinner of Alaskan King crab legs and fresh Maine lobster, and we used the first pair of Sea Scissors off the production line. They went through the shells like butter."

When asked if she had a food fantasy, she said, "To repeat our New Year's Eve 2000 dinner – this time with lots of family and friends."

We did just that.

Mother and Brother Get Sick

While living in Wyckoff, New Jersey, we built a house in Cape Coral, Florida for my mother and brother Jimmy. Unfortunately, they only got to enjoy it for a mere three months. My brother, at the age of fifty-five, was diagnosed with bladder cancer. My mother had congestive heart failure. She had contracted rheumatic fever when she was only fourteen years old, leaving her with a weak heart. The doctor had actually advised her to not have children – she ignored him and went on to have five.

Her condition was not life-threatening at this point, but she was certainly not getting any younger. Over time, her heart began to get worse, slowing her down considerably.

My mother and Jimmy called us and asked, "What should we do?"

We decided to have them move in with us. After all, we had plenty of room. My brother was in so much pain I sent my nephew down to Florida to bring them back to New Jersey.

Jimmy's cancer was becoming more aggressive, and Janice took care of him as well. At three in the morning one of them would be moaning, and we would both start to wake up.

"Go back to bed," Janice would say. "You need to be at work at 7:00. I can go in whenever I want."

Then she would assist them to the bathroom or do whatever else was needed. She was their caregiver ninety percent of the time. My contribution was more like ten percent. She took care of them like they were her own mother and brother, while working a full-time job. She truly did everything that one person could do, probably even doing the work of two or three caregivers. She was phenomenal.

Janice was also involved in my mother's dialysis process. She went to school to become certified so she could do the procedures from the comfort of home. Our house was suddenly crammed full of dialysis equipment and medical supplies. Ultimately, my mother never had to leave the house again; to her relief, she did not really have to go anywhere at all.

There's a phrase that comes to mind – they say a mother can raise five kids, but five kids can't raise a mother. Well, Janice and I took on the job. If the truth be told, Janice took on the job like a champ.

I couldn't have been more thankful and proud of her for doing so.

Finally, the time came that we had been dreading. My brother's health was clearly failing. I called my sister and told her that hospice said the end was probably coming that night.

I also called Eddie and let him know what was happening. He came over with his girlfriend at the time, and that's when Jimmy was pronounced dead. Eddie called the funeral parlor for me; that's how tight we were at one point. We would do anything for each other. He was truly my backbone. When I needed something or was in a tough position, he was there for me and I was there for him.

Jimmy died on my nephew's birthday, September 17, 1996. Within nine months, our mom followed him on June 24.

It was a tough time, because I also lost my uncle, who was my godfather. I shared a birthday with him. He had six children and lived in Florida. They had his body shipped to New York, and I went to view it for positive identification.

He had died of cancer, and sadly his head had gone from the size of a bowling ball to a peach. You could tell it was him, but he had clearly gone through hell. They could not shut the coffin fast enough for me.

These losses were devastating to me, but luckily I had Janice, who showed me everyone stays with us in spirit. Deep down, I knew they were now in a better place.

Janice Gets Sick

In 2002, Janice retired at forty-five, only to be hit with breast cancer.

We were planning to move to Florida when she decided to have a mammography. The doctors didn't find anything wrong with her, so we went forward with our plans. Not long after we found a place, Janice didn't feel well.

"Something's wrong," she said.

We scheduled an appointment with her gynecologist back in New Jersey, who confirmed that there was nothing to be concerned about. "You're going through your changes and your breasts are starting to harden. That's all," he reassured her.

But when we got back to Florida, she could not push the worries away. "You know," she said. "I just want to get another mammography, just to make sure."

This time we set up an appointment in Fort Myers. The results come back. Once again, the doctors told us there was nothing wrong.

In June, we were back up in New Jersey, visiting family.

Janice said to me, "I want to go to the doctor. But I'm not going to go to a gynecologist again. I'll set up an appointment with Dr. J., our family surgeon. He saved my mom's life."

"How long have you had the lump?" Dr. J. asked Janice.

"What lump?"

"There's an extra bulge there."

When we told him that Janice's doctors had given her a clean bill of health, he examined her again. He then told us the tumor was as big as a grapefruit. "Alright, we're going to get you tested. Just go to Passaic General tomorrow, and I'll have everything set up for you."

The following day, it seemed as if Janice went through every test possible: scans, MRIs, blood work...everything. The prognosis wasn't good.

"I scheduled you for surgery," Dr. J. told Janice.

She took the news in stride, but the prospect of having only one breast alarmed her.

"I need to have two breasts when I wake up. Can you recommend a good plastic surgeon?" she asked.

"One of the best in the country has a practice close by. He works in New York and Montclair. I'll arrange an appointment for you."

To Janice's relief, the plastic surgeon told her he would be able to reconstruct her breast. When she had adequately healed, he would then tattoo a nipple on to it.

"Everything went well," Dr. J. told me after her surgery. "But we need to wait for the results."

A total of twenty-three lymph nodes were removed from Janice's breast – all twenty-three had cancer.

With aggressive chemo, they gave her two years to live. Determined to beat the odds, I researched breast cancer and its treatments. When I discovered pomegranate juice was exceptionally high in antioxidants, I made sure she drank the POM brand daily. I prepared healthy meals from other foods high in cancer fighting abilities. In addition, I had her take an assortment of vitamins. If I thought it might help her live longer, I made sure she had it.

When we went to Hawaii for our fifteenth anniversary, I arranged to have her pomegranate juice brought to our table every day so she could have it with her breakfast. It worked miracles, in my opinion. Pomegranate juice and all that extra care helped her live for another eleven years. Nine years longer than expected. We were given the gift of more time. I kept on researching, and Janice kept on living.

The hospital staff called her the miracle child. "If the cancer was in twenty-three lymph nodes, it's amazing she's still alive," they said.

Our next step was to set up an appointment with an oncologist in New Jersey who wanted to look into stem cell options for Janice. He was hoping to enroll her in a clinical study at the Hackensack Hospital because her cancer was so advanced.

But Dr. J. was against it, "No, no, no, no, no," he said, "you don't want to do stem cells. We only do that as a last resort. You need to do a radiation and chemo regimen to stop the cancer."

At one point, she had received so much chemo, her breast started to leak.

When she had a consultation with the plastic surgeon to repair it, I said, "Hey, doc, how about if you tie it in a knot then loop it around like this," I demonstrated. I guess years of tying threads into knots while fishing had given me the idea.

"If what I'm doing doesn't work, we could give it a try," agreed the doctor. After he attempted the standard procedure twice, with no success, he tried what I had suggested. It worked. "You should get your medical degree," he joked. "And then come and work for me."

"No," I said. "This is just for my wife. I'm not working anymore."

Janice's condition seemed to improve, so when her doctors took her off her current medication, we were concerned.

Eight years later, the cancer was back. And once it came back, we were told there was no chance of her surviving.

"You might want to consider celebrating Christmas a bit early," the cancer specialist told me in October. "Because she might not make it to the end of the year."

I continued to do everything I could for her. And she lived another three and a half years because of it. I don't know what it was, but I thank God.

Not long after, we went to one of her doctor appointments and took the elevator to the fourth floor. Even though the waiting room was overcrowded, Janice didn't have a chance to sit down.

"Mrs. Seaman, they're waiting for you," called out the receptionist.

They said that they would monitor Janice's care from Sloan Kettering. Unfortunately, we never had the chance to continue the treatment.

Years of doctor's visits and tests. One doctor says this, but the other one says that. All of this had put Janice on the defense.

She told the doctor, "You can do anything you want, but you're not drawing my blood."

She was done being pricked with a needle.

The doctor ran what tests he could, and then gave us the results. "You have at least five to ten years. We might even have a cure by then."

Here's the real kick in the ass. Five days after receiving this good news, Janice died.

We left the doctor's office in high spirits, thinking everything was going to be all right. We stopped for a celebratory dinner and drink. During our drive home, we were dancing, singing, and talking. We were on top of the world.

I looked over at her and could tell she looked a little tired.

Concerned, I said those dreaded words. "Something doesn't feel right."

Maybe all the excitement had worn her out, but just to be sure I began asking her simple questions such as "What day of the week is it?" and "Who's the President?"

To my relief, she was able to answer correctly, but I continued to question her every hour or so. When she answered accurately, I gave a sigh of relief.

"So, she's good," I thought. "She's just worn out."

But by the time we arrived home, Janice was so weak she could barely get out of the car. She could hardly put one foot in front of the other. I walked her into the house and helped her into bed.

In the meantime, I asked her sister to come over and help. Luckily, she only lived a mile away.

"A woman should be here, just in case." I told her. "After all, anything could happen. She might need to go to the bathroom or something."

Chemotherapy had left its toll on Janice and was slowing destroying her immune system. Unbeknownst to us, sepsis – a life-threatening illness that can be triggered by an infection and can shut down the organs – was kicking in.

"I'm just beat," Janice said. "You can't imagine how tired I am."

By noon the next day, Janice was so weak I rushed her back to the hospital. Knowing chemo can really knock the energy out of you, I figured she probably needed a pint of blood.

"Her kidneys are shutting down," we were informed. The doctor didn't seem overly concerned. "If her kidneys fail, we'll put her on dialysis to clean the blood. We'll start first thing in the morning."

Seeing that all the equipment was ready, I said to the doctor, "But you've got everything. Why don't you start now?"

"No, she should be fine," he replied. "As long as her blood pressure is steady, we can wait."

But they had waited too long. In the morning, Janice's blood pressure had dropped and was too low to start dialysis. They could not drain her kidneys, and they started to shut down. When the kidneys stop working, your body fills with extra water and waste product, essentially drowning you. We lost her at 3:21 in the afternoon. She died on my sister's wedding anniversary. The same day as my sister had lost her husband a year before.

On our last night together, Janice had said to me, "I could never live a day without you."

I should have known something was happening then. You know, we were very happy. They had given her five to ten years, and now here I was, saying my condolences to everybody in her family. It was crazy.

Allen Starts Dating

People don't realize just how lonely it can be when you are a widower. You go out with your friends during the day for lunch or shopping, and it's all a good time, but when you arrive home at nine or ten in the evening, there's nobody there. All you can do is sit and stare at the walls, thinking about what you used to have and how you don't have it anymore. It's so lonely.

You could go out, go to bars, and pick up girls, but that's not very fun. That's not what your heart wants. You want to share your life with someone you love. Someone you can do all the little things with – jump in the pool, go to the beach, swimming. I didn't want to do those things alone. I wanted to have someone I could snuggle up with while we were watching a movie. It's the simple things. I wanted someone by my side shopping for the ingredients for a new recipe we wanted to try and then eating our creation together. Someone to have a few laughs with, you know, stuff. Janice and I had fun every day, and we had so many good times together. But suddenly I was alone. I didn't have anybody to run to. There was nobody in my family, really. After all, we had no children.

My sister's husband died a year before Janice, but she had three adult children and two grandchildren. She never had to live alone. Shortly after her husband died, she moved in with her son and said, "I'll be your babysitter."

I had everything from a big house to a boat in the yard, but I had no one to share it with. You know what I mean? And it was lonely. It really was. Here I was in a fifteen-room house – and it was completely empty except for me. I was just sitting in a 5,000-square foot house talking to myself. I just needed somebody to sit and talk to. It would have been nice just to have somebody there. There would be days when I would cry myself to sleep.

There were times I was ready to go.

I would talk to my nephew once in a while. He'd come over and I'd say, "Barrett, this is killing me. All this sitting here alone, it's driving me crazy. If this doesn't change soon, there's going to be something happening to Uncle Al here. I'm not going to put up with this garbage much longer."

My sister, Judi, was worried about me. So was my friend Lavonne from Indiana, who happened to be a therapist for the church. They saw that I was going crazy sitting alone at home. I didn't have anybody, a woman, or even a friend.

I lived like that for two years and was going bananas. Lavonne and Judi warned me that I was becoming depressed and had to do something about it. They suggested I join Our Time, a dating website for people fifty and over. Both told me they had only heard good things about it.

I was a bit reluctant at first and decided to date an old acquaintance instead, hoping it would get me back into the swing of things. After all, I had not been out on a date in thirty years! Besides, I liked the fact that she was a Jersey girl.

Diane and I started dating but only saw each other once every few weeks because I lived in Florida and she lived in New Jersey. We were having a great time, but after only three weeks she was talking about marriage.

"Well, we'd have to work things out," I said as we talked it over. "It sounds like a plan, but let's see how it goes day-to-day because I like our relationship as it is right now."

Even though I didn't want to rush into it, marrying her did seem like a good idea at the time. Since we had already been friends for a couple of years, I figured we wouldn't have to wait that much longer. After all, how much more time did we need?

"Next summer you can move into my house, and we'll live together," she planned excitedly. "Then when I retire in a year and a half, we'll move down to Florida to your house."

But in the end, she got cold feet.

The long-distance relationship thing was tough on me, and I wanted to spend as much time as possible with her when I was in New Jersey. As a result, I think she thought I was too controlling.

She was divorced and kind of vengeful. She would wait for you to make a mistake and jump all over you. Or if you were right too often, she would say, "Oh, so you think you know it all."

Little remarks like that would come out of her mouth all of the time. We started to fight every other day. One day we would have an argument and the next Diane would call me up, acting all nice and sweet. It was very confusing, I practically had whiplash. As I was not provoking her in any way, I kept trying to figure out what exactly was going on. But there really wasn't a logical explanation. It was simply her mentality from being with her first husband; it's no wonder they got divorced. She even started an argument over ice cream once. I mean seriously, it was vanilla or chocolate. Pick one. We're going to argue over frigging ice cream? No, no, no. This will never work.

"This one's driving me crazy," I confided to Lavonne one day. "I don't know if I can do it."

"Well, get rid of her. Get rid of her now."

"Yeah, I think you're right. Maybe I should," I replied.

Then all of a sudden, she posted something involving a friend on a social media site. It rubbed me the wrong way.

Upset, I asked her, "Why did you do that?"

"I can do whatever I want," Diane replied. "I'm single."

That didn't sit well with me. I'm not that type. If you say something that's going to make me look bad in front of my family and friends, it affects me.

"I never did anything wrong to you – ever. I always put you on a pedestal. I don't think this is working out."

"No, I don't think so either," she agreed.

"Okay, good. So it's over."

So I went back to Florida. Afterward, we had a couple of fights over the phone, calling each other back and forth to bust each other's chops. This went on for a month when I decided to send her a text message. It was the lyrics to the old song, "I Can't Live Without You."

Well, within fifteen minutes, eight cops with their guns drawn surrounded my house. It looked like the SWAT team was invading my lawn.

"You've got to be kidding me?" I thought.

Evidently they thought I had a gun and was either going to kill myself or shoot up the neighborhood.

The cops called me up and said, "Would you please step outside?"

When I opened my front door, they told me to put my hands up.

I laughed in disbelief and asked them, "What the hell's going on?"

"We received a phone call," one of the officers said to me. "We were told you were thinking of harming yourself."

"Let me guess," I said. "It was a fifty-seven-year-old woman from New Jersey."

Somehow she had misinterpreted me texting the lyrics into I was about to kill myself.

The cop started laughing and said, "Yeah, how'd you know?"

"Look," I said, "here's the story. Do you guys want to come in?"

As I'm inviting them in, I see even more officers emerging from around the fence and behind the trees. Holy shit, they don't mess around. It really was like the SWAT team was here.

The cops come in, and they could see the house was clean and orderly. We sat around my kitchen table, which had some donation envelopes on it ready for me to bring to church on Sunday.

"I guess you're not planning on killing yourself?" the police officer said.

"Not today," I said.

After telling him the full story, we start joking around.

Finally, he simply said, "Women. Don't ever take this one back. Do not answer her phone calls. Do not reply to her texts. We deal with this every day, and these people are going crazy. Stay away from this one. Find someone else."

These guys were hysterical. Before I knew it, we were shaking hands and becoming friends. They hung out for a while, and then they left.

I took their advice and was relieved to have Diane out of my life.

That incident caused me to listen to Judi and Lavonne and try out Our Time. Ultimately, it turned out to be a great site because I would meet the woman who would eventually become my wife. My life would be fantastic again. Unfortunately, Debbie was not the first woman I met on it.

***

When I first joined, I needed to write an entire script about myself, my hobbies, what I like to do for fun, if I like dogs, and if I smoke. Everything. I was asked to write what I was looking for. It took me some time to find a date because I had a detailed list of what I was looking for in a woman. I found a couple who came close.

I thought, "I'm not getting desperate here, but I want to go out with somebody."

Finally, I connected with a woman I wanted to meet, so I met her for lunch at Bahama Breeze in Fort Myers. Nice lady. She was very attractive, very good looking for her age. I thought she was really pretty. We were having a nice time when all of a sudden, she started picking on the people around us and saying nasty things about them. I kept the rest of the date cordial, but I was thinking this is not your typical laid-back Floridian. We said our goodbyes.

She asked, "Are you gonna call me tomorrow?"

"Yeah," I told her. "I'll give you a call."

I waited a day or two. But when I texted, she never replied.

A month went by, and then out of nowhere, she started texting me again wanting to go back out.

"Why haven't I heard from you in the last four weeks?" I asked her, "You could have reached out at some point."

It was the last time we talked.

She's probably still on Our Time because, let's face it, she's a bitch. Really, who cares what someone looks like or what they are wearing? Just mind your own business already. Enjoy the weather, the water, and everything around you! Some of these women were so negative. If they could just relax and be themselves, it might have worked out.

***

My preferences were clearly stated on my Our Time profile. "No tattoos," but that didn't seem to matter to another woman I met. There we were at Naples beach when she pulled up her little sweater only to reveal fourteen tattoos on her back.

"Why?" I asked her. "You knew I didn't want to date a woman with tattoos."

"Well," she said, "I was hoping you would change your mind once you met me."

"No, I'm sorry," I said. "I just can't deal with that. I'm not one of those guys who likes that kind of stuff."

Call me old fashioned, but I don't like tattoos on a lady. I just don't get it. After that one date, we called each other a couple of times, but I was not interested in seeing her again.

***

Then I dated yet another woman from Naples. We planned to meet at this nice Italian place on the water for lunch. When I arrived, I noticed a woman walking toward me in the parking lot. She flung her arms around me and started kissing me on the lips. I had never met her before in my life.

"You're Allen, right?" she said after the fact.

"Yeah," I said. "Good thing you got the right guy."

You should have seen her. She was wearing a see-through shirt.

"You know," she said, "I wore this for you."

Yeah, me and how many other guys?

Before I knew it, we were sitting in the restaurant. She was having a glass of wine quickly followed by another. It was only one in the afternoon, and I watched in disbelief as she ordered her third glass of wine.

"Come on, let's go for a walk," she said.

It was a nice, sunny day on the water, so I agreed.

"I want to show you something," she said, leading me into this building.

As I headed upstairs, I could hear live music playing. It was a beautiful sky-bar, and we sat on the rooftop overlooking the Venetian Bay.

"Why don't we order a drink?" she suggested.

"Sure," I said. "You only had three or four already in the past hour."

Pretty soon, she was all over me. And her tongue was in my ear. Drunk, she started telling people we were married.

"You are nuts," I said, cracking up.

"What's the big deal?" she said. "We're never going to see them again. Who knows, we might get married. It's none of their business."

She was about ten years older than me, but it was funny how she did whatever she could to keep me smiling and laughing. It felt like she was trying too hard and none of it seemed natural. When our date came to an end, I walked her to her car.

"Goodbye," I said.

Well, she started to kiss and hug me again.

"Listen," I said. "You're not raping me, honey."

I laughed because she was acting like she was eighteen.

"You know, I'm thinking about taking you home tonight."

"No way," I said to myself. But out loud I said, "I have my own car, and I'm not going to your house tonight."

She was a real wacko and called me every day for the next five or six months. Even if I told her I was dating somebody else, she still called. She wanted to see me again and was texting me sweet messages. Although she was nice, she was a bit too forward and fast for me. Her fondness for wine was also a little too much.

***

Not long after dating the wine-consuming woman, I was back on Our Time when I came across this really attractive girl.

"Oh, this one's cute," I thought to myself. "Nice, innocent, good-looking girl."

I sent her a message and we connected. After a few conversations, we agreed to meet for dinner at P.F. Chang's. Well, the girl in the picture did not look like the girl in the parking lot.

When I saw this girl get out of her car and head into the restaurant, I looked at her ass and said, "There should be a license plate on that because it's so frigging big. That can't be the girl from Our Time."

Guess what? It was her.

I was like, "Holy mackerel!"

She looked like 120 pounds in her picture, yet in real life, she was more like 240. Obviously, the picture was not recent. On the internet, she looked and sounded so nice. In fact, when we talked and were planning to meet, I had suggested, "Why don't we make it a weekend-long date?" After all, she was off Friday, Saturday, and Sunday. So, we agreed on a marathon date, which I now wanted to cut very short.

While at the restaurant, I learned quickly that if you bought some of these women an eight-course meal, those eight courses were gone. She ate like crazy. My date ate so much food, I felt like me and five guys probably couldn't have kept up.

"Did you want dessert?" I asked her when she had finished.

"Well, we could have a little something," she replied.

We bought this giant chocolate cake, and she killed ninety percent of it.

"How in the hell did she do that?" I wondered.

The way she just kept eating and eating, I was lucky to even get a bite. She was an eating machine.

On Saturday night, I cancelled. "I ain't coming back," I said to her. "I'm not coming to see you again."

"Okay," she said. "I didn't think you were working out for me."

I replied, "I'm glad you thought so, honey."

***

My next dating experience was with a woman from Sarasota.

On our first date, she said, "My son's getting married in May. Would you be my date at the wedding?"

"We just met an hour ago," I said.

As if she didn't hear me, she said, "I'd like for you to meet him. As a matter of fact, he's here on vacation with his fiancée and a friend or two."

I didn't know what to say, and the next thing I knew we were going around St. Armand's Circle, hitting every bar and restaurant looking for her son. Now, as I've never met him, I have no idea what he looks like.

Finally she finds him, and the first thing he says is, "Ma, nice guy. Is he coming to the wedding?"

I was going crazy. What's with this family?

Then she asked me to marry her after only dating for three or four weeks – to marry her! To say I was dumbfounded would be an understatement.

One afternoon while barbecuing at my place, a neighbor came over, needing my help.

"Please watch the barbecue," I told her. "I'll be back in five minutes."

"Yep. No problem," she said.

When I returned, it was obvious she never left her chair. All the food was burning on the grill. I gave her a look and shrugged my shoulders in a way that said, "What the hell?"

"Oh, did you mean for me to do it now?"

"Why would I ask you to do it later? Of course, do it now. But just stay there. I'll take care of it."

We ate in awkward silence.

Then I told her, "You have got to go home."

It escalated into a fight. I was tired of her crap and slammed the door, saying, "Goodbye, I don't care to see you again."

***

Although I wasn't having much luck in the dating world, I continued to meet people from Our Time. I met this real nice girl from Bonita Beach. Really nice. We met in October, and she asked me to marry her in early November. I met the whole family for Thanksgiving; I mean her brothers, sister, nieces, nephews, cousins – everybody. We had a beautiful dinner, and her family made me feel very welcomed. Her mother and father adored me.

Her father even said to me, "Well, I hope to see you again."

"Sir," I said, "there's only one person that's going to stop us from seeing each other, and it's your daughter. If it was up to me, I'd be buying breakfast for everybody tomorrow."

That night, she texted me a picture with a message saying, "I'm glad you're in my life. I love you. I can't wait to live with you."

Well, that was the last day I saw her. I was very confused, but it turns out I was right. She did stop us from seeing each other.

A little bit later, her sister contacted me. "She got cold feet," she explained. "Allen, you should call her and try to talk to her."

"Why? What did she say?"

"She said she loves you, Allen, but she's afraid."

It was weird. We got along so well. She was a smart girl who attended Purdue University, but she knew how to push my buttons. She would go so far and then pull back a little bit. She had a little bit of money, so she sort of lived in fantasy land. I wanted a girl who lived in reality.

Her last message to me was, "I'm grateful that you're in my life. I'm so happy that we met, and I love you with all my heart."

That freaked me out. If she was so in love with me, why did she push me away? I couldn't understand that.

All of these dates were taking a toll on me. It looked almost hopeless. Then I met Debbie.

Debbie & Allen's First Date: *His Side*

I think of that song – "Two Less Lonely People in the World."

After meeting a couple more "not-all-together-there-women," I deactivated my account. A short time later, Judi and Lavonne convinced me to go back on.

"You just have to give it more time," they told me. "The right one is out there waiting for you."

I'm glad I took their advice. A week before Christmas, I came across this cute-looking girl on Our Time. Her picture and biography were really sweet, clean-cut, and fun.

"Well, we have a lot in common so far," I said when I saw that she was a widow with no children.

I did notice she was Jewish. Having never dated a Jewish woman before, I didn't know much about the religion.

"But what the hell," I thought. "I'm in my fifties and people are people. Why should I give a damn about something like that?"

I called her up, and we started talking. I told her about my experience of meeting women who didn't quite look like their picture.

"Well, I'll send you some recent ones," she said.

"Yeah, could you? I'd really love to see what you look like today, not what you looked like twelve years ago at your prom or whatever."

She laughed and sent me more pictures of herself. Wow! This girl could have been in Hollywood. She had herself all set up nice and pretty in her bathing suit! I knew that I had to meet her.

Besides looking great, she was a lot of fun to talk to and had a good sense of humor. She was the real deal. Not picking up on any red flags, I decided right then and there to give dating one more chance.

We spent Christmas Day talking on the phone and making plans to meet for the first time on New Year's Eve.

During this conversation, she took me by surprise by saying, "I've got to ask you a question, but it's personal. I really feel bad asking you."

"You know what," I said, "my life is an open book. Ask away."

"Are you circumcised?"

I didn't know what to say. I'm like, "What? Where is this coming from?"

"No, really, are you circumcised?" she asked again.

"Yes, of course," I answered.

"Oh, that's good, because you know...I'm Jewish. We don't like that uncircumcised stuff."

Now this is a girl who had only been with one man her entire life, and she's giving me a spiel. I'm cracking up. And if I wasn't circumcised, we weren't going to date. That's what she told me!

Debbie picked Jane's on Third restaurant in downtown Naples for our first date. When I arrived and walked toward the place, I saw this nice-looking girl sitting outside.

"Hey," I thought, "I wonder if that's her."

She was close enough to see me but wasn't looking in my direction. I watched her for a few seconds from about ten feet away, when all of a sudden, she pointed at me and smiled.

"Is that you?" she asked.

"Is that you? Yeah, that's me." I smiled back.

"Oh, my God."

People were watching us, and I went over and gave her a little kiss on the cheek. Oh, she was so nervous! She blushed and laughed like a nervous school girl.

She hadn't been on a date in maybe thirty-seven years. I had more experience thanks to Our Time. Of course I wouldn't really call some of them dates, if you know what I mean. They were...how should I say it? Entertaining.

We walked toward the entrance and got a nice table for two right next to the koi pond that had a water fountain in the middle of it. The restaurant was set up beautifully, and it just felt like everything was falling into place. We didn't plan anything. It was a great time. It was a great first date.

About ten minutes into our lunch, I could tell she was still very nervous.

"Wow," I thought. "Reality's kicking in. She's on her first date since her husband passed away."

"Honey, everything is going to be okay," I said, placing my hand on her arm. "The worst that could happen is we have lunch and go home. Or we could have a nice evening and see where it goes from there."

She relaxed right away. In fact, we were holding hands at the table, asking each other, "Do you want to share something from the menu?"

It was a perfect day weather-wise. After finishing our meal, we walked hand in hand to the pier. Debbie put her arms around my waist, pulled me close, and kissed me.

"Wow. First date, huh?" I thought to myself, laughing. "I wonder where this is going."

She had a sexy walk. However, it wasn't until later in our relationship that I found out she had a foot problem. Her wiggle was actually a wobble. It's our little joke.

We were having a great time. We just laughed and laughed.

A car pulled up next to us, and this guy yelled out, "Go get a room already!"

Debbie was so embarrassed, but she never let up. She was still holding me, hugging me, and kissing me.

While we sat and enjoyed the view from Naples Pier, this young woman in her twenties came up to us and said, "You guys are so in love."

Deb and I exchanged a quick glance at one another and blushed.

"I've never seen such a happy-looking couple in my life," she continued. "I passed you three or four times, and the way you are holding hands and talking to each other is so sweet. Can I take a few pictures of you?"

We never met this woman before in our lives, but I'm glad she took those photos. I cherish those memories.

The fireworks were scheduled to start around seven thirty, so we made ourselves comfortable on a nice bench. Debbie didn't tell me she was afraid of fireworks! Every time one of them went off, she jumped half a mile.

"It's just fireworks," I tried to reassure her. "When you see the lights go down, you know you're going to hear a boom."

Even so, she just couldn't deal with the noise. She repositioned herself, burying her head on my lap, and freaked out.

After about ten minutes, I said, "If you want to leave, we'll go for a walk back toward town."

She nodded gratefully. "Yeah, come on. Let's go."

We continued to hold hands as we walked back.

"It's almost nine," I said. "I think I'm going to head home."

"No," she said. "You're going to stay at my house."

I took a breath. "First night and you want me to stay over?"

"Yes," she said. "You see all these drunks on the road?"

"Yeah."

"Well, I live only a few minutes away. Follow me."

"OK, but on one condition. I get my own room."

I explained that I had been talking to my two personal advisors: my sister Judi and my friend Lavonne. They had specifically told me that if Debbie was a nice girl and I stayed over, we needed to sleep in separate bedrooms.

Debbie nodded. "That's right; we won't do any of that stuff. You will have to be a gentleman."
"Yeah, but that's going to be a little different for me. That's not my scope of life, you know?"

"That's not a problem," she said, "but I should tell you that I have a little dog."

"Whatever," I said. "I love dogs. We'll have a good time."

It was a little after midnight by the time we were ready for bed.

"Alright, now where's my room?" I asked.

"You still want your own room?"

"Yes," I confirmed.

She showed me to my room, and I locked the door. I began settling in for the night, when all of a sudden, I heard the doorknob turning.

"I just wanted to make sure you had everything," Debbie said.

"You're full of shit. You want to come into my bedroom!"

I had to crack up at that. I didn't go to sleep for hours; I was laughing so hard.

Okay, I will tell you the truth. She really didn't want to come in; she was just making sure that I was comfortable and had everything I needed. I didn't have an overnight bag with me because I hadn't planned on staying over. The night passed, and I slept great, even though Rosie, Debbie's dog, kept scratching at my door.

Debbie made me breakfast in the morning.

"Wow, this is really nice," I thought. "She cooks and the house is immaculate. Everything is perfect...even her dog's nice."

In case you're wondering what happened next? I'll tell you – she turned on the radio.

"Oh, I wish 'A Beautiful Morning' would come on. Do you know that song?" I asked Debbie. "Janice's cousin actually wrote it."

But, nah, it didn't come on. So we listened to a Rascals' song on her computer instead. She still plays Eddie's music today. We listen to it all the time, whether we're getting ready to go somewhere or if we're just staying home and relaxing.

I went home after breakfast, but it wasn't long before she called me up. In fact, I was only home for about two minutes when my phone rang.

"Are you okay? Did you make it home?"

"Yeah, I just got here."

"Okay, I just wanted to make sure."

We stayed on the phone for a while when she said, "Come on back tonight. We'll go out for dinner."

"It's an hour drive. There, back, and back again."

"So what? Stay over," she insisted. "You've got your own room now. And you know how to lock the door."

We were laughing. This whole thing was great. I even had to call up my sister and Lavonne to let them know. "We slept in the same house, but different rooms. Don't worry. I locked the door."

"Good. You're a gentleman. She must be really nice."

"And we have a lot in common," I told them. "The weird part is that we talk about our spouses like it's nothing."

When I dated those other women from Our Time, it seemed like they were still brooding over their divorces and were trying to get even for what their spouses did to them.

When one of them came to my house, she said, "You have pictures of your wife all over the place? I don't want to see that. Oh, they have to go."

I was like, "No, you have to go."

Even though I was a widower, they were still insecure about the fact that I had been married before. Some of these women even wanted Janice's urn out of the house. But Debbie could not be more different. Today, at our house, we display photos of our spouses freely. We are comfortable with each other and want to keep those memories.

Most people think that is beautiful. But there's a few who look at the photos and ask, "Why would you do that?"

It simply works for us. In fact, we can't wait until we have a three-bedroom house, because one room is going to be ours, one's going to be Janice's, and one's going to be Paul's. One will have Yankees stuff on the wall, and the other one will have Mets. I joke with Debbie, telling her Janice's room will be nice, but I'll probably have to spray paint the walls in Paul's room or something because of all the Mets memorabilia.

We're living and having fun, and we talk about our spouses every day. We even call each other Paul or Janice once in a while by mistake. We don't even blink anymore when we do that.

It'll be like, "Hey, Jan, could you get me an iced tea?"

"Sure, hon," Debbie will say without missing a beat. "I'll get it."

Things were progressing well, and we were certainly enjoying each other's company. Only a few days after our first date, Debbie called, sounding very upset. She was having a tough day.

"My dad's dying," she said between a few sobs. "And Paul's gone and my mom's gone.... I'm having an emotional time."

"Alright," I said. "I'll be there in forty-five minutes."

"Really?"

"Yeah. I'm packing a little bag in case you need me to stay the night."

"You're wonderful. You don't know how much this means to me."

"Wait a minute," I said. "What am I going to do? Not help you? Go somewhere else?"

I reminded her that I found a nice girl who I like and have a lot in common with.

"We're only nine days apart, birth-wise. We're both widowers and have no kids. So you need somebody. I need somebody," I went on from there. "It's like that song, 'Two less lonely people in the world.' That's us."

"You know, this is about the third or fourth date, but I already think I'm falling in love with you."

"Good," I said. "I'm glad you said it first, because you don't know how happy I am."

I was so content. We could sit down and watch a movie, go out to dinner, go wherever. We were just like a married couple.

People would ask us how long we've been married. I had to laugh and tell them, "Well, we've only been dating for about two weeks."

"Get out of here," they would respond.

What can I say? When you have found the right one, you know it.

"Wow, thank God I was ready, huh?" Debbie said with a smile.

"Yeah, thank God you were."

Allen Meets Mo

Debbie was crying.

"What's the matter?" I said, rushing to her side.

She looked at me with tears in her eyes. "My dad's sick," she said. "We've got to go see him."

Debbie had mentioned before that I reminded her of her father because we had the same attitude and talked alike.

I met Mr. Levine at Naples Community Hospital. He was a nice guy, and we hit it off right away. "You can call me Mo," he assured me.

"Sorry, I can't," I said. "I'm not that way."

I'm old school and wasn't going to call him by his first name.

I got to meet him a few more times before he passed away. We talked a lot and joked around. He was living in a senior home in Naples. One day, while at his place, he was lying in bed and could hardly move.

"Mr. Levine," I said, "one thing you've got to know. I love your daughter, and she'll be taken care of the rest of her life, as long as I'm alive."

"Thank you," he said with gratitude.

You could see he was instantly relieved. He knew somebody was going to take care of his little girl, his only child. He died three days later.

We were at Debbie's doctor's appointment, only to find out that she needed heart surgery, when we got the call.

"Your dad is on his way out," hospice informed us. "He's only got a couple of hours at best."

We ran out of the office as fast as we could and got there with about an hour to spare. As he lay dying, Debbie talked to him. I was crying like a baby. I couldn't believe how strong she was, especially knowing the news she had just received from her own doctor.

When we left his room, I told her, "I don't know how you did it. I would have been on the floor, dying, crying with him."

"Well, what are you going to do?" she said with a slight shrug.

In my opinion, she didn't have time to grieve her mother or her husband, and now her father was gone.

Debbie started to feel as if she was jinxed. She even said to me, "Maybe you ought to think about leaving me. Everybody who loves me has died."

"We'll turn that around," I said. "One, two, three strikes they're out. Now you have a new guy. It's a whole new program."

This made her smile, something she had not done for the past few weeks.

There are a lot of customs and traditions in the Jewish religion for when a loved one dies of which I knew nothing about. I didn't know what to expect. I didn't know if her family was traditional, or if they had to sit Shiva and all that kind of stuff. But I still wanted to be there for her.

"If you want, I'll go to Rhode Island for the funeral with you," I offered.

"You would come with me?" Her face brightened. "I don't want to go alone," she confessed. "But we can't let my family and friends see us together."

It had been less than a year since Paul had passed away. Debbie didn't want family and friends to know that not only was she dating, but things were already getting serious.

"Okay," I agreed. I backed her one hundred percent – whatever she wanted done, we were going to do it.

Debbie wanted to be sure her father's body had arrived safely, so we viewed the body together at the funeral parlor. Then before her family arrived, she dropped me off at the hotel and went back to attend the services. I understood the situation.

I got to meet some of her family a few days later. To this day, I call her uncle my Uncle Bernie.

When the cousins are on the phone with me, I always ask them, "Hey, how's Uncle Bernie doing?"

They seem to get a kick out of that.

I'm like, "Why not?"

He's a nice guy; he's Debbie's uncle. He's Uncle Bernie to me. We have talked plenty and had some great conversations. The guy is business-minded and has invested his money wisely. He sure knows a thing or two about money and has reaped the benefits. Maybe that is why the two of us get along so well. He's always asking Debbie and his daughter, Shari, about me to make sure I'm doing okay.

As far as some of the other family members go, I met some of the other cousins. I thought they were ok. It's like I always say, "You can't pick your family, but you can pick your friends." That was one of the best things about our marriage, making new family members to call my own.

Actually, I think one of her closest friends was a bit jealous that Debbie found such a nice guy. She was also single and about our age. She tried dating and found out that guys either wanted her money or just a fling.

After we tended to her father and took care of arrangements, we went back to Debbie's doctor.

He told us, "You can't wait much longer. You need to get the surgery done."

"Alright," we agreed.

We picked out a surgeon in Philadelphia. The guy was one of the best in the world.

Before scheduling her surgery, Debbie said she wanted to talk to me about something.

"Shoot," I said.

"I think we should get married."

"Sure. Tell me whenever you're ready, and we'll move to the next step."

She truly couldn't love me anymore. It was just unbelievable. I could see where we were headed.

I said to her, "I don't know about your feelings, but I'm going to tell you mine. If you want to go to the next level, you do the talking. I know where I stand."

"Okay, good. Will you marry me?"

"I thought the next level was engagement. But now you want to get married?"

"Yeah. We don't have to wait long, do we? You know, we're both adults."

It was a serious topic, but we both started laughing. Man, we just couldn't stop.

"Yeah, well, we are adults. But you have got to be kidding."

"No."

We were in love, but there were other factors for us to consider as well. Debbie wanted to get married for legal reasons, in case medical decisions had to be made.

"Sure, I'd marry you. Why not? When I look at everything so far, we sure are having a lot of fun."

"Okay, that settles it."

We went on to get married in April and let everything take its own course. Just like that. It is amazing how fast life can unfold in a whole new direction.

Lucky Twice

Debbie & Allen
Their Story

The Wedding

When Debbie and I first met, we had an ongoing Monday lunch date at Tin City. Then we would walk to Fifth Avenue to grab an ice cream or coffee and stroll along the street. One day, we stopped in front of a real estate office to look at the homes displayed in the front window. We decided to go in and inquire about some of the homes and get information. Looking back, I'm not sure why we did this, since we had only been seeing each other for a brief time.

Maybe it was serendipity because Annie, the real estate agent, became a very special friend. She was a savvy and successful business woman and we began to talk about real estate with her. She assumed we had been married for a long time because we were so comfortable with each other and was shocked when she learned we had only been dating a couple of weeks.

We went to lunch with her on a weekly basis. She didn't pressure us into buying a house, but it was fun to look at all the beautiful homes after our meal. We would fill her in with our weekly updates, and she would share our story with her friends and coworkers because they found it so fascinating.

I believe it was Annie who first said to us, "You need to write a book... this would make an incredible movie."

After that, everyone we told our story to said the same thing.

One day, we were on a double-date outing with our newfound friends, Annie and her husband, Kyle, when Anne steered the conversation directly at me. "Have you told her you love her yet?"

"Of course," I said with a smile, "but she said it first – and she asked me to marry her."

We laughed.

Her next question was straight to the point. "Can I go to your wedding?"

"Sure, but we don't have a date yet." I looked at Debbie and suggested, "What about the first of April?"

"Really?" said Debbie.

"Why not? Everybody's going to think we're fools for getting married so early, you know?"

Needless to say, she agreed. We planned a private, quaint little wedding at the Naples Beach Club. We asked Georgia, a friend of mine, to marry us. We thought that would be a nice personal touch.

Coincidently, Debbie's friend, Rhonda, would be vacationing in Naples in late March.

"Hey, if your girlfriend's around, why not ask her to be your maid of honor?" I suggested to Debbie.

"But what about Barbara?" she said. "I already asked her."

Barbara's husband, Bobby, was going to walk Debbie down the aisle (actually the sand, as the wedding was taking place on the water's edge). Barbara was one of the first women Debbie had met at the Naples Newcomers Club. They joined roughly around the same time and clicked immediately. Debbie told me Barbara was always there for her after Paul died. As a matter of fact, they were playing Mah Jongg when Debbie and I first connected online. Barbara was so excited for Debbie. I later found out she had texted Debbie during our first date, so if she wanted to get away, Barbara was going to call with an "emergency." Fortunately, that didn't happen.

"So, you can have two maids of honor. What's the big deal? It's your wedding day. You can do whatever you want."

"Rhonda was my maid of honor at my first wedding."

"Even better," I said. "Why don't you have her at your second wedding, too?"

"Yes, I'd love to, but she's leaving the day before."

"Don't worry, I'll take care of it," I said. "The only thing that matters is making sure you can have your friend there."

We changed Rhonda's flight and even arranged for a limo to drive her back to the airport after the wedding.

Not sure how our families would react, we decided to limit our guest list to a small group of friends. Even though I had some family in the area, I didn't share the news with them. Debbie didn't tell anyone either. So when we tallied the number of people attending, there were nine of us in all. However, our private wedding attracted all kinds of spectators on the beach. People were clapping and whistling as if this was a wedding for the rich and famous. Debbie wore a nice sundress and held a matching bouquet. As we stood hand in hand with our toes in the water, my friend officiated the ceremony. We did it!

We were married!

Following the brief ceremony, we had a nice reception right there on the wet sand of the beach, just five feet away. We sat back for a beautiful lunch and wedding cake. A friend of Debbie's, Sarah, is a professional cake decorator. Not only was the cake delicious, it was magnificent. It was entirely edible with seashells, sand, water, and beach chairs. It was perfect.

Then at the end of the night, it was just the two of us...finally.

We ate in the glow of the tiki torches on the beach. It was very special because Naples Beach Club only allows one couple a day to do this. Debbie and I felt like a queen and king being served by our personal waiter and busboy while the host took pictures. We held hands as we watched the sun set into the ocean. It was gorgeous, and a wonderful memory.

Our photographer wanted us to go down by the water for pictures.

People cheered, "Go, go!" They were really going crazy and clapping.

We started to kiss. It was really a great time, simply a beautiful time. Our evening came to an end when we went to our room around 11 PM. We could not have asked for a better day.

Everything was perfect. The day after, we texted and called family and friends to share our exciting news. I sent a picture of our wedding bands to my sister, Judi, without saying a word. I just sent it to her in a text.

She responded with, "Yeah, what?"

"We got married."

"Get out of here. It's April Fools. Ha ha."

I called my sister the following day, and she still would not believe me. "Yeah, you're still doing April Fools' jokes, ha ha."

By the fourth of April, she still didn't believe me. "Let me talk to Debbie," she demanded.

"We really got married," Debbie told her.

"Get out of here, you really did? Congratulations! You guys are nuts!" She paused for a beat. "Wow. It has only been three months."

"Yeah, I beat you," I said. "You only knew your husband for four months before you got married."

Debbie and I were laughing. It was like nobody believed us.

***

Our honeymoon was wonderful. Debbie enjoyed swimming, so she fell in love with being in the Gulf every morning. We spent our time walking the beach and sipping drinks. Breakfast was always room service, but we ate our other meals at the hotel restaurant. It was like being on an island somewhere, just the two of us. The funny part was, even though it was a very exotic location, we were only a mere twenty minutes from home. It was really nice, just beautiful. The weather held out, and we had a great time. We didn't want it to end.

After our honeymoon, we went to Debbie's house in Naples. Although she loved my house, at over 5,000 square feet, she thought it was way too big. She was much more comfortable in her own cozy home. Plus we had Rosie to take care of.

***

I'm grateful to have met Deb. I'm glad I waited and things worked out the way they did. She was worth the wait. She was the only one who was a person of her word. Whatever she said, we did. Whatever I said, we did. We never changed stories; we never made excuses. We did what we wanted to do because of each other, and it was great. It still is great. It's fun. It's just like my first marriage, just a little different. We have been very happy from the beginning. I tell everyone I was lucky twice. Deb tells everyone that she was the one who was lucky twice. I don't know how to say it, but it's like it was meant to be. We hit it off so well so fast, and we were there for each other. If we didn't have each other, what would we have done?

Debbie's Surgery

I had a big secret to tell Debbie before we got married. I was worried about her reaction.

"We have an issue," I said.

"What is it?" she asked.

I told her I loved her, and she told me she loved me too.

Then I took a deep breath and said, "I had prostate cancer."

It was one of the hardest things I ever had to tell her because I knew it was what Paul had died from. I had to make sure she understood what she was getting into.

I explained that in 2006, I was diagnosed with prostate cancer. Two years later, I got the news I had kidney cancer. Luckily, I never had to do chemo, only radiation on my prostate. My left kidney was removed, and my cancer has never returned.

In some ways, my prostate cancer was worse than Paul's. He had a Gleason Score of six and only lived for a few years. A level of six or seven is essentially a death diagnosis. Mine was a nine, but I'm going on twelve years now. It was a lot to put on Debbie, considering what she had already gone through. She had to take a few days to really think it over.

She was hemming and hawing when I finally said to her, "I would understand if you want to back out."

I took a step back and put myself in her shoes. I asked myself what I would do if she had breast cancer. If my heart told me to be with her, then that is where I would be. Nothing else would matter.

I even asked her, "Did I leave you over your heart issue?"

"No."

"And now here I am, wanting to be with you. And I'm cancer-free."

She considered this and said, "Well, you haven't had cancer in about nine years now. Yes. I think we can do it."

"You're right," I told her. If she wanted to do it, I knew we could do it. "We can do anything, especially together. What do we have to lose?"

A month after our wedding, we went back to the doctor.

Debbie's cardiologist asked her, "So, how are you feeling after surgery?"

"I didn't go yet," she said.

"Are you kidding me? You were supposed to have this taken care of this."

He yelled at her – which is good!

I agreed with the doctor and said, "Well, if that's what he told you, you've got to listen."

"I had a reason," argued Debbie. "If you weren't going to stay in my life, I wasn't going to have the surgery."

Determined to find the best surgeon, we began making phone calls across the country. Money was not an object when it came to our health. That's the way I looked at it.

One doctor we liked was Dr. B., who had a practice in Pennsylvania. His surgery and staff were fantastic. The hospital was state of the art, and I felt even more comfortable about our decision as soon as we walked into the facility.

"Your valves have expanded and are leaking," he told us after running all kinds of tests. "It looks pretty bad."

He went over what the procedure would entail and told us what needed to be done on our end.

Prior to Debbie's surgery, I had what would be my last 4th of July cookout at my house. I always looked forward to it because my yard offers a spectacular view of the city fireworks. Usually when I hosted this cookout, I'd have close to 150 people show up. However, this year I wanted to keep it small because it was my first party after marrying Debbie. We invited only a couple of close friends and relatives. Unlike our first date, she could enjoy the spectacular fireworks because they were farther away and the noise was not as deafening.

A month later, we were back in Philadelphia for Debbie's five-hour operation. I asked my sister, Judi, if she would drive in from New Jersey and stay with me until Debbie was released. We are so grateful that she was there for us.

I was beside myself because the doctor had emphasized just how serious the surgery was. "You can't imagine," is what he said.

"Okay," I said, "but you're doing it, so, I don't have to worry about her, right?"

"Yes," he reassured me. "She is going to be fine."

Debbie, on the other hand, was concerned that she might not pull through. She asked me to make sure Rocco's urn would be placed in her casket. I wasn't sure how to go about planning a Jewish funeral, let alone the protocol of burying her beloved pet with her.

She started to explain all the different traditions including, "You've got to wear a yarmulke to go see the body," and so forth. But I was too wracked with fear to comprehend it all.

"Is there another option?" I asked.

She shook her head. "Call my cousin Shari. She'll know what to do."

That was a good idea because Shari had helped Debbie with her father's arrangements by connecting her with a Rabbi and Cantor.

So here I was in Philadelphia, with Shari's phone number in one pocket and Uncle Bernie's number in my other pocket. I was just plain worried, but I tried to put on a brave front for Debbie.

"We've got this beat," I told her. "There ain't nothing you and I can't handle, as long as we do it together."

She went into her surgery like a trooper. For the life of me, I couldn't figure out how the hell she was staying so strong. I'd be crying, not knowing the outcome. It was rough to imagine her on the table with all those tubes stuck in her. If I woke up with all this stuff on me, I'd be yanking it off and getting the hell out of there.

While she was in recovery, the doctor came to see me. "Mr. Seaman, I would like to show you something."

"What?"

"I want to show you pictures of her valve. She wouldn't have lasted two more weeks."

I couldn't believe the size of the hole around her valve. I'm no doctor, but I could tell how serious her condition was. Thank God, I got her to listen to her doctor.

"She shouldn't be alive," he said bluntly. "Her valves should have blown out."

I was startled, but he kept right on explaining.

"Your artery should only be an inch wide. Her artery, however, was three to four inches, enlarged and leaking. They were ready to burst."

All I could say was, "Holy crap."

He texted me the photos, so I could share them with Deb when she felt better.

On the second day after surgery, they got her up and walking. By the fourth, they were ready to send her home.

"I'm afraid. I am not ready to leave," she insisted.

They allowed her to stay on an extra day. And when she was released the following morning, we checked into a nearby hotel. Debbie made bypass surgery look like a walk in the park, especially after what she had been through. She was amazing.

I have pictures of her in recovery when I thought, "Oh God, we have a long way to go from here."

But she proved me wrong.

When I showed them to her, she said, "I don't remember a thing. I just don't believe it. It's incredible I lived through that. Guess I'm kinda lucky."

"Yeah, you sure are. You don't think you're strong," I said, shaking my head. "You're one of the strongest women I know."

During our stay at the hotel, Debbie grew stronger each day. After her two-week follow up, she was ready to go home. But the doctor suggested we visit some relatives and friends in New Jersey, because he wanted to follow up with her in a week's time.

We took his advice.

When we went back, he gave us his OK. "You're doing fabulous. You're way ahead of schedule," he said. "Go home."

"Wow," I said. "That's because you had a fantastic caregiver."

I smiled at Debbie, taking all the credit.

"See you next year," the doctor said.

I was confused. "We don't have to come back?"

"She's doing great. Everything is done."

They actually replaced her valve with a cow valve.

Now every time we see a cow commercial, I ask her, "Honey, are they relatives?"

Or if we pass a farm, I say, "Honey, they're having a family reunion. You weren't invited?"

Sometimes she starts laughing; sometimes she gets annoyed. It cracks me up at least. Either way, she knows that I care and love her.

Now you wouldn't know anything was wrong by looking at her. She seemed great and still does today. She can do anything she wants and puts me to shame, even outdoing me sometimes. I'm trying to hold back and not have her overexert herself, but she's like, "No, come on, let's keep going."

That's my Deb.

Married Life

I am the only man Janice had ever been with, and Paul is the only man Debbie had been with. For some reason, one of the things I like about my life is I've only had two loves – Janice and now Debbie. They're similar, yet different too. I'm extraordinarily fortunate to have had time with two women who share the same morals, ambition, and heart.

I can still vividly remember introducing Debbie to my family for the first time. We went to see Cousin Eddie, and some of Janice's family was there. At first, everyone was walking on eggshells and acting super nice; it was truly over the top.

"Just be yourselves!" I thought. "Don't be phony bastards."

I knew it was a bit strange and sad for them to meet my new spouse, but they accepted her. I was grateful. They could not have been any kinder. Janice always made me smile, and they could see Debbie was making me smile too, something I had not been able to do since losing Janice.

As I mentioned before, some of the women I dated took offense to Janice's pictures and urn being displayed in my home and wanted me to remove them.

So I asked Debbie if this would bother her.

"Absolutely not," she said.

We never leave Janice and Paul out of our lives. As a matter of fact, Debbie's bridal bouquet had two white roses alongside her purple flowers, one for her and one for him. White roses signify those you have lost.

Now that we are married, we have pictures of Paul alongside Janice's urn in our bedroom. Debbie will jokingly talk to her, asking how she put up with me for all those years. I do the same to Paul's pictures.

We even talk about having a "Paul room" and a "Janice room," so when guests visit, they can choose which one to stay in.

***

I am truly blessed Debbie would do anything for me. I remember waking up in the middle of the night in excruciating pain from kidney stones. This was extra worrisome because I only have one kidney left. Debbie was awake instantly and took me to North Naples hospital, practically driving 110 miles an hour.

A few months later, I had three hernias taken out.

During my recovery at home, I would be laying on the couch and say, "You know, do we have any ice cream?"

Within thirty seconds, there was a bowl of ice cream with whipped cream and a broken cone in my hands.

I was like, "Holy cow!"

"Would you like something to drink? Do you want a snack? Do your bandages need changing?" Debbie would ask, making sure I had everything I needed.

Unfortunately, I soon developed a strange protrusion in my stomach. It felt like something was ripping inside of me. I went back to the doctor and was told it was fluid buildup and to give it time. When I returned, he tried to drain the fluid, but nothing came out. After examining me closer, he informed me that the hernia mesh had come undone and explained he would have to perform a more invasive surgery in order to fix it. I had to stay in the hospital a couple of nights, but Debbie was a trooper. She stayed by my side the entire time, even sleeping in my hospital room.

But that is how we are; we are each other's caregivers.

There are so many stories about Debbie that bring a smile to my face.

One day, when we were walking down Fifth Avenue in Naples, I passed gas.

She looked at me like she's such a proper lady or the Queen of England.

"What?" I said.

"How could you do that?"

I looked at her. "You never?"

"Not in front of you. And when I do, they're roses."

"Bull. Your ass stinks like everybody else's."

Sometimes it's like we are ten years old and everything is simply funny. Every once in a while, we'll be in bed and I'll nail her with a good one and pull the sheets up over her head. Once, we were laying there with the fan on, relaxing and talking. I had some bad gas. I'm telling you the truth, it's embarrassing, but it's funny as hell. Debbie farted too and almost peed the bed because she was cracking up. Our legs and arms flapped in the air while we tried to suffocate each other with our "roses." It was so hysterical. We couldn't stop laughing and started to cry. We were like two kids acting ridiculous, but that is the relationship we have. And we enjoy it.

When Debbie and I first started dating, I was around 210 pounds and she told me I looked really good. That was seventy pounds ago, when I was called "the new meat of Naples." It was a good market to be in for single guys. In season, I've heard it's seven women to every man; it's practically a dating service just walking down the street.

Luckily, we're out of that racket.

The only problem we have now is our love of eating out. Believe it or not, we don't mind that we've put on a few extra pounds. I think Deb looks even better today than the day we married. To us, it's a sign of being healthy, happy, and in love.

I always do my best to go with the flow. A friend of mine advised me to start each day thinking of a way to make Deb happy. I follow that advice every morning.

I ask Debbie, "What do you want to do today?"

Our habits have changed as well. Deb never used to watch much TV, but now we binge on Netflix – everything from Royal Pains to Hawaii Five-O. She will even come to bed and call me by the names of the characters on the show, but I don't mind. Even something as simple as watching TV is enjoyable with her. I truly look forward to it. We aren't the type to join a fancy country club, but we do try to stay active. Sometimes we'll go to a baseball game or just stay home and relax. As long as I'm with her, that is all that matters. We're soulmates; not just best friends. We are husband and wife.

A Typical Day

I'm never in a rush. If I had my druthers, I would stay in bed until two or three o'clock in the afternoon. What's the rush? We're retired. Life is good. Relax.

Deb, on the other hand, used to wake up at six ready to hit the ground running. Now she often sleeps late, sometimes not getting out of bed until ten o'clock. Something I have brought out in Deb is the ability to unwind. She has mellowed out to the point where she can now enjoy a rainy day in bed.

There is no need to rush and put unnecessary pressure on yourself. Tomorrow is another day. And God forbid, if you die, somebody will do whatever you didn't get to.

I think the only problem in our marriage, if you want to call it a problem, is we are too laid back. In the morning we'll shower, do some chores around the house, and then have breakfast. From there we'll sometimes do a bit of grocery shopping or go for a drive around town or along the beach. Then we see how the day unfolds; maybe we'll go to the mall or take in a movie.

When the weather is really nice, we might spend more time at the beach, walking out on the pier or strolling through downtown Naples like we did on our first date. We can have fun just grabbing a cup of coffee and people watching.

At dinnertime, we will go out and try a new restaurant or make something together at home. Debbie told me she cooked elaborate meals for Paul every night. And her friends and family all mentioned what a wonderful cook she is. Ha.... I haven't seen many home-cooked meals.

She did make a wonderful baked stuffed shrimp dish while we were still dating. It was stuffed with crab meat and crackers. Since I loved it, she made it again after we got married, and I told her it didn't taste the same.

She tried it and started laughing saying, "I'm sorry, but I forgot the crab."

It was just cracker stuffing. I guess Paul lucked out, and I got the short end of the spatula when it comes to Debbie's cooking.

We'll often take a swim in the pool at night, and then we generally watch some television before we head to bed. There's no rush, there's no pressure. We love keeping things simple. If our house seems a bit lived in, that's because it's not a showpiece. It's our home.

We try to take nothing for granted and appreciate each day. There are so many things that you have to do in life that you never in your wildest dreams pictured yourself doing – like taking care of our parents when they got sick. We know that each day is precious and try to live it to the fullest. We need to remember this when it comes to our own health ailments. Some of my family members can be such drips and would make the worst of an already stressful situation. I mean, you have to keep your sense of humor and deal with it. You've got to make the most of life and have fun because it's all too short.

Future Plans & Staying Thankful

We know we will encounter challenges from time to time – my kidney stones, two hernia surgeries, and Deb's heart surgery. And that was all within the first year of our marriage! There are many wonderful things about growing older and accruing wisdom, but the health challenges can be painful.

No matter what, though, I am grateful to have Deb in my life. When Janice died, it felt like everyone left my side. I am not sure if it was the new reality that I was a single person or if they didn't know how to best support me throughout my grieving, but it was lonely.

I think our relationship works because we have this connection of having a love lost and a new love found. We understand that a tragedy isn't the end of life. There is always a second act if you are open to it.

We tell ourselves all the time – we are lucky twice.

We recently bought a beach villa. And although we are not the country club type, there is one close by that we are thinking of joining. However, our friends and family are taking bets on how long it will be until I get kicked out. It's hysterical. We keep things exciting and dynamic through our shared love of travel. We planned a driving trip for about six to eight weeks, heading out to Texas including stops in New Orleans, Biloxi, San Antonio, Arkansas, Tennessee, and Kentucky...all the way up to Chicago. But that was just a warm up. We have other road trips in mind, such as a drive up the Eastern seaboard from Florida to Maine. Sure, it's a lot of time on the road, but there is nobody else who I would rather do it with. We are only on this earth a short time. Why wait?

In the years to come, we might go even farther – from here to California, up to Washington, through the Dakotas, and then back down through the middle of the country again, all the way back to Florida. We are looking forward to it because it will be a journey together. Deb has already seen every state in the country since that was a goal of Paul's, but they mostly did it via airplane. It will be an entirely different journey by road.

It may not make sense to hit the road when we have our houses to take care of. Sometimes it can be a lot easier to just stay home. But in the end, we will always be happy wherever we are. We have learned from our stories that life is not guaranteed. You truly never know what it will throw your way. Just when you think things are looking grim, you find someone incredible to embark on a new journey with.

I haven't been this happy since being with Janice. It's a continuation from my heart. We laugh every day, and that might be the key to our happiness.

We are lucky twice.

Epilogue

This book was written not only to tell our story, but to encourage others who have lost a love one and to let them know it's possible to find happiness again.

Remarrying may not be the answer for everyone, but find the thing that will bring you happiness again. Then get up every day and move forward to whatever that is. Remember, the person you lost wouldn't want you to suffer.

Everyone experiences sorrow in their own way, and there is no timeframe for grief. Never allow others to dictate what you need to do or allow them to disapprove of your choices. It's your life; you do not need negative people in it. Healing doesn't mean you forget. Take care of yourself, be kind to yourself, grieve when you need to, but remember that life does go on and there can be happiness and a smile on your face again. Thank God.

www.luckytwice.net